BE NOT SOLICITOUS

Be not solicitous therefore saying, What shall
we eat: or, What shall we drink: or, Wherewith
shall we be clothed?

For after all these things do the heathens seek.
For your Father knoweth that you have need of all
these things.

Seek ye therefore first the kingdom of God and
his justice: and all these things shall be added unto
you.

Matt. vi. 31-3

BE NOT SOLICITOUS

*Sidelights on the Providence of God
and the Catholic Family*

Edited by MAISIE WARD

THE CATHOLIC BOOK CLUB
121 Charing Cross Road,
London, W.C.2

THIS EDITION 1954

ACKNOWLEDGMENTS

We wish to thank *Integrity* for permitting us
to reprint several of the stories in this book.

PRINTED IN GREAT BRITAIN BY
LOWE AND BRYDONE (PRINTERS) LIMITED, LONDON, N.W.10

CONTENTS

PART I: The Family

Plea for the Family   MAISIE WARD   3

PART II: Families

Babies, Bills and Mr. Blue   WILLIAM GAUCHAT   57

Our Two Families   MOLLY WALSH   70

Abandonment   J. E. P. BUTLER   87

Flight into Egypt   D. H.   95

Our Child is Mentally Defective   ANONYMOUS   111

The Young Familiar Faces   WILLIAM WALSH   116

Stripped for Action   PAUL ZENS   142

A Red Brick Schoolhouse   GRACE ELIZABETH ROGAN   148

Six Aren't Enough   BILL MORGAN   159

Marriage and Spirituality   MARY REED NEWLAND   171

An Interracial Catholic Marriage   NANCY DU BOIS   186

The Joy of Poverty   "MRS. J."   194

Marriage for Keeps   ED WILLOCK   208

Postscript on Poverty and Marriage   ED WILLOCK   246

BE NOT SOLICITOUS

PART ONE

The Family

PLEA FOR THE FAMILY

ᏋᎯᎧ

MAISIE WARD

I

READING any daily newspaper you feel how deeply imperilled is that ancient institution the Family: plans for education of the child, for his feeding, his playing, the care of his health and his teeth, his whole vocational equipment and training as a citizen, are more and more independent of, separated from, the family unit. Not by totalitarian rulers only but by all governments the pressure is increasing towards treating the child as belonging to the State and reducing to vanishing point the responsibility (to say nothing of the authority) of the parent. And parents seem very ready to co-operate with the State in this matter: accepting the State school and its outlook, rejoicing in the fact that the child's play hours too are handled in groups of his fellow-scholars, that almost all his waking day is outside their ken.

"It's lonely for him at home," the parents of one child very truly remark. And small families are the order of the day, divorce the remedy applied when husband and wife cannot live happily a life which they have almost

3

emptied of the great purpose which should keep them together.

And yet . . . and yet. . . . Have you ever made a long journey by plane, train or boat and fallen into casual conversation with the man in the next seat on the plane or the neighbor assigned to you in the ship's dining room? And how long was it before he pulled out his wallet and showed you pictures of his wife and children? Love of family is one of the deepest natural feelings: Père Loew has told us out of his wide experience as a priest working among the workers of Marseilles that not even the most brutalizing conditions of life, overcrowding to a point of horror, insufficient food, inescapable filth can altogether destroy a man's love for the baby his wife has borne him. The family is the primary unit of a natural society, and nature is hard to kill.

There are other things you can read today—more in periodicals than in the daily press—straws some of them, indications merely that the wind is shifting its direction a little, others more serious pointers, but all pointing the same way. There are magazine stories of children in anguish for fear their parents intend to divorce, of girls or boys growing up totally unable to adjust to life because of the broken homes in which they had first awakened to it.

Some of these stories are doubtless fiction, but these fictions are the mirror of fact. Statistics collected by social workers show the overwhelming proportion of problem children coming from broken homes. I have myself been in touch with two schools, one for delinquent girls, the other for backward and ill-adjusted boys. Almost all these children were the children of divorced parents.

Social workers are increasingly bidding us fix our eyes on these facts. During the blitzing of London they noted that children evacuated to the country away both from the bombing and from their parents suffered far more from nerves and unhappiness than did those who remained with their families, slept in shelters and shared all their dangers and miseries.

In Chicago a number of young divorcees have discovered the fallacy of Chesterton's ironic ending for the modern fairy story, "They were divorced and lived happily ever after," and have formed themselves into a group to work against divorce. Calling themselves "Divorcees Anonymous," they offer to meet and talk with women who intend to break up their marriages, that they may tell them of their own experience, and persuade them at least to wait. One or two divorce court judges accepted this offer, and at the end of a year the group was able to say that it had mended fifty marriages which had appeared hopeless.

In these new discoveries of old truths: that children need their parents, that husband and wife need one another, that the family is of nature's ordering, human beings are going along an old road of establishing truth by seeing the results of denying it. But this road is a long and hard one, and as man walks it he sets up for himself almost impassable obstacles against the moment when he will seek to retrace his steps. Society has, in other words, been built today on so many false assumptions that it has narrowed human life and made exceedingly difficult the living of it in a human fashion.

What are fifty marriages saved in the ocean of Chicago's divorces: and will they even stay saved?

What are the two lovely children that travelling salesman proudly showed me, to the five he might have had if he were not living in a tiny apartment among other families all limited to one or two? What is that fragment of home life of his, compared with all the wealth of a possible family life, when the home houses the older generation and the young bring their friends into it instead of always going out, when families are grouped in communities with a pattern of aid and service "mutually careful one for another" (I Cor., xii, 25), "the whole body being compacted and fitly joined together" making "increase of the body, unto the edifying of itself in charity" (Eph. iv, 16).

Here Saint Paul is speaking, and he is speaking in an age whose thinking was not unlike our own, an age too in which man had lost the pattern nature shows, had followed every turn and twist of inclination as our society has, had erected most of the same hazards against its own return and others besides, had felt itself powerless to retrace its steps and knock down its obstacles even when seeing that they were creations of its own folly.

I was told lately by one who moves in a sophisticated intellectual circle that all the talk today is of original sin. "Probably," my friend said, "they got the idea from Graham Greene." Wherever they got it, "the idea" is a useful one, because it is an idea that corresponds with reality. It brought Chesterton into the Church, because it explained humanity and was the starting-point for dealing with it. It must too be the starting-point for dealing with a situation created by it, and for considering God's remedy for it in human life. Sin answers the question of humanity's failure to make its paths straight by natural means and to build a satisfactory natural community. And it leads us to think of that new supernatural community Saint Paul is speaking of. "Just as the human body," wrote Pius XI in his encyclical *Casti Connubii,* "is formed by its members, so the city is what it is made by the families and men of which it is composed."

And Christopher Dawson writes: "If the Catholic theory of society is true, the supersession of the family means not progress, but the death of society, the end of our age and the passing of European civilization."

II

Communism has been far more successful than Western Democracy in awakening youthful enthusiasm. It has offered a vision to the boy and girl of a world of peace and unity, it has harnessed the spirit of self-sacrifice, brought together young people from all over Europe, and from China and Korea besides, into a unity that seems a strange, distorted reflection of what Christian unity ought to be. In many newspaper articles we are shown the faces lit with fanatic enthusiasm, the marching and the banners with Stalin's face where Hitler's used to be—the hatred formerly vented on the Jews now directed against America. We know something of how this has been brought about: of the Communist "secret weapon" of youth training and indoctrination, above all of the vision they have managed to hold up to the young. And we know too how lacking in vision has been Western Democracy in countering Communism —because Western Democracy has lost its own vision.

Communists have indeed a vision but we Catholics have, or should have, *the* vision. What means have the Democracies of countering the quasi-religious enthusiasm awakened in these boys and girls? Various suggestions are made, some a little quaint, such as plays of

Shakespeare at Stratford-on-Avon. Surely there is a depth and width of historical, cultural and above all religious knowledge needed before these plays can even stir their minds. Another suggestion is to bring together the young, especially the young leaders from all the countries that remain free. But what are they likely to gain from these contacts (even when the language problem is overcome) except an exchange of information on baseball against information on cricket!

No. What is left of our Christian heritage is at once too good and not good enough to offset the Communist appeal. It is not good enough where sport has become the one authentic thrill of youth, it is too good where its ancient culture still calls for a preparation of the mind and that absorption by the whole being which can only come of *living* in a certain society. Again, it is not good enough where it offers no vision calling upon the depths of love, but it is too good where it refuses to call out the passion of hate.

For these rallies of Communist youth are built upon hate as much as, more than, upon love. Communist unity, like its Nazi predecessor, is kept only by outlawing and hating part of humanity. These boys and girls are not healthy in their marching and their singing: their eyes and their voices show fanaticism, they move to a rhythm of mass hysteria. You cannot cure hysteria by changing its direction. You can only cure hysteria by health. True, it is natural to the young to get together and shout—at a football match or at a rally. But such getting together, such shouting, can only be one element in life, the spontaneous expression of fellowship and enthusiasm. And even a football match occasionally reveals the tendency to hate in human nature.

The element insufficiently stressed in most descriptions of Soviet youth is the religious nature of the Communist appeal: the only answer to it that has ever really met it has been the religious answer. The only international that has ever begun to succeed is the Catholic International. The Young Christian Workers have gathered in their hundreds of thousands and have known a deeper and more authentic thrill than the Hitler Jugend or the Stalin marchers.

Yet here too there is a danger which we must face if the Christian Community is to be rebuilt in our day, a danger of which we seem curiously little aware. If we are answering Communist youth by Christian or even merely Democratic youth, we should remember that Communism first copied the Democracies in this odd isolation of one element in a community. It was a weakness of nineteenth-century social and religious work that it always grouped the objects of its attention by age and by sex. Today we still see this in the structure of our parishes: men's clubs, women's clubs, boys' clubs, girls' clubs. Children of Mary, Knights of Columbus, Men's Communion Day, Children's Mass. The family has been split today, not only by its enemies the Communists but by its friends the Catholics. Not intentionally of course. Taught by the Church to prize family life, we never dreamed that by following the common pattern of our age we might be weakening it. Our eyes were fixed upon certain objectives: the children must learn their doctrine, they must go to a Catholic school; we were willing to pay, to make sacrifices for this end. So much the better if the school in turn took off our hands these other problems of their worship and of their leisure hours—in a good Catholic atmosphere. It was far better equipped than we were to teach, to guide, and likewise to amuse. And so, bit by bit, we parents let go our responsibilities, and in so doing, loosened if we did not lose, the structure of family life. A profound thinker and a holy man, Fr. Vincent McNabb, once said with that explosive energy that was his, "Far better if all the millions spent in England on Catholic schools had been used in equipping parents to teach their own children."

Saying this, he neglected to reckon with the State, which insists on school-going. But he might even have meant that a fully Catholic home with fully instructed parents could make their children capable of passing unscathed through State schools. I heard lately of the president of a society of Catholic women who, asked about the Catholic attitude on some important matter, said, "I would not have the impertinence to answer such a question. I referred it of course to our reverend Moderator." Some parents appear to have almost the same attitude about teaching doctrine to their own children. I wonder at what stage we members of a teaching Church become able to say that we have learned enough of her teaching to impart it to our neighbors and friends, to say nothing of our children?

This is a parenthesis, but it is an important one in relation to the atomizing of the family into a number of individuals of different ages.

Somehow we must get back to conceiving the family, not the individual, as the unit. It is too easy for the State to absorb the individual; it is too easy for propaganda, for waves of enthusiasm, to sweep off their feet masses of the young. For the young are naturally conformist: they like to dress alike, to do the same things, to think the same thoughts as all around them. Hence it is all too easy for either Communism or any other ideology to sway them in masses. The absolutely necessary counterweight must be found in the family, in the balance it gives between generations, in its possession of treasures of wisdom and tradition lost in the impersonal school and in the paternalistic State.

But until Catholics themselves return to a full realization of what this means, the Catholic family will do but little. In France, the Young Christian Workers began a splendid apostolate. But when the first generation married and became parents they soon learnt that to continue the techniques they had been using got them nowhere: they must re-think the problem, they must re-group: the unit must now become the family. In such countries as Poland and Hungary where the old traditional pattern of Christian living had been kept, not reflected upon perhaps but simply followed generation after generation, the only chance for Totalitarianism was to break that pattern by breaking up families. Read the tragic stories of the deportations: fathers and mothers separated, their children torn from them. After ten years Catholic agencies, both papal and American, are still trying to reunite families torn apart in that first frightful year when Stalin, then Hitler's ally, carried off into Russian lands hundreds of thousands of Poles.

III

There are, as we have seen, indications today that the pagan world around us is discovering that its road of social experiment has been to some extent a road of error: that an effort must be made to restore the stability of society through stable families. Even more is there among Catholics a drive towards re-discovering the fullness and richness of the supernatural community, through exploring all that is contained in the Christian idea of marriage and family life. Family-life study groups, Cana conferences, retreats for married couples, the Catholic Rural Life Movement, the Christian Family Movement, the Liturgical Revival are all increasingly centered on the family.

Who that has heard him can ever forget Mgr. Ligutti, of the Rural Life Movement, talking to a group of school-girls and drawing on the blackboard the average rural family: father and mother followed by six children; and then the average urban family with one child and half a child pathetically tottering in the parents' wake!

For one of the main causes of this atomic civilization of ours is that it is urban: it is in rural areas where the pattern of a community made up of families has persisted that the dictators have found the strongest internal resistance, it is in our towns that faith, morality and all purpose in life crumble under the assault of an unnatural way of living that fights against life itself. "It has been well said," Christopher Dawson remarks, "that the great city is the grave of a culture."

But we cannot all "flee to the fields" (Fr. Vincent once chose these words of Scripture for the title of a book). And, although many of the stories in this book of ours are bound up with the decision to find in the country health and strength for children and a fuller home life for a family, it is possible for the Christian family to hold its ground also in the cities. It is far more difficult. Landladies refuse "children and dogs," flats grow rapidly too small, neighbors complain of noise, tidy clothes are needed for daily use, prices seem to soar as the growth of the family makes daily expenses more and more serious: where can the children play safely in the streets, when can they have fun without annoying somebody? I know one mother who had to carry two heavy children up and down several flights of stairs to get them out to a park for a few hours' play—with a third tumbling down and stumbling up as best he might. And then, sitting in the park, her mind was tormented over the pile of unwashed clothes and dishes, the unswept floors, her husband's supper to be prepared when all this other work should be behind her. A house and garden rank as a luxury in the city: for a young family they are almost a necessity. Small wonder that mothers in city apartments grasp eagerly at kindergartens and pre-schools as solving for part of every day the problem of where to put the children while the work gets done. Small wonder that a fourth child looms as a terror.

This particular mother used to take with her milk, fruit and bread and butter. She fed the children out there and waited in the park until her husband came back from work. He too was tired, but he helped her to collect the family, and while she was rapidly tidying up and getting supper he struggled with the bedding down of the babies: two in the tiny room that was too damp to sleep in when winter came, the third in their own inadequate bedroom. They were both worn out, and for the hundredth time they thrashed out the question: Can we move before the winter? And for the hundredth time they answered it: Not without a down-payment for a house.

But they did move before the winter—leaving their flat to a couple with only one child, who in turn were deeply thankful to move from the single room where they had been eating, living and sleeping. This was made possible by a friend who lent the money for down-payment on a house, tiny indeed but with back and front garden, a small bedroom for the girl and another for the two boys. Whenever they went out, the mother told me, the little girl begged her to hurry home for fear the new house should have vanished away.

Like all the stories in this book, this story is a true one and should be far commoner than it is. The restoration of the Christian family can never be done by any family alone: they cannot lift themselves by their own boot-straps. The whole Catholic body must become aware of this problem. This book is called *Be Not Solicitous* because its theme is the Providence of God in relation to the family that puts its trust in Him. But God's providence works normally through human instruments. Those of us who have any money to spare are morally bound to help those who in our present abnormal society are struggling back to the norm of family life. "Where economic and political questions are concerned," said Pius XII, speaking to a group of French parents, "families may be in very different circumstances and sometimes strive with or even oppose each other. Here an effort must be made—and Catholics are responsible for giving the example—to promote equilibrium even at the cost of sacrificing individual interests for the sake of internal peace and healthy economy."

The attempt "to promote equilibrium" may in these days especially call for gigantic efforts and heroic sacrifices: it certainly calls for an earnest consideration of the world we are living in. One American parish adopted a displaced family. One parishioner found a job for the father, others paid the fare to bring them, women made curtains and gave bed linen: another group got together a down-payment for the house, others collected furniture. And all welcomed this new family into the vital fellowship of a living parish.

The mother of a spastic boy was talking one day with a friend who proclaimed herself an atheist. "I don't see," this woman said, "how you can reconcile it with your duty to your boy to spend so much time working for underprivileged children. Surely your one duty is to earn all the money you can and put it by to support him after you die."

The mother answered, "If I don't do this work it won't be done, and I believe that if I help these children God will take the more care of my child." The atheist waxed scornful at this idea, but later she remarked, "You don't deserve it, with all your foolish notions, but I'm going to tell you for your comfort that I've made my will and I'm leaving £1000 to your boy."

"There you are," my friend answered her, "God."

"Why on earth," said the startled atheist, "would God have anything to do with me, when I don't believe in Him?"

The phrase "playing Providence" is usually understood in a bad sense. Neither parents nor friends can take God's place in guiding and shaping lives. But they may well be His instruments, so that the easing of burdens and the provision of air and space for the growth of a family may be willed or refused by another family.

We are truly at a moment when the survival of the family threatened by the social atmosphere, threatened by State absorption, must be insured by the effort of the whole Christian community.

Next to the housing problem is that of maternity care. I have visited families where the mother was not only home from the hospital in less than a week but was already obliged to do all her housework and handle three, four or five other young children. There would of old have been unmarried sisters or aunts who could have moved in and helped, but today a girl must sacrifice her job and perhaps a cherished career if she is to be available when she is needed. Here, too, better-off families can help by paying someone who could not afford to work for nothing to carry the mother's burden for a few weeks until she has recovered her health and strength.

Naturally enough, perhaps, it is always the poor who help the poor. One story in this book tells of a family, whose house was partly paid for by a perfect stranger whose entire savings went into it and who only asked that they should do likewise if they were ever in a position to do so. Short of this, the tendency is on the increase for families who are intensely concerned with family life to get together in close-knit groups to help and hearten one another: to take turns in "baby-sitting," to buy co-operatively, to exchange worn clothes according to size and sex among their children. A wider co-operation in ideas and mutual help is achieved where the written word can be used to draw together like-minded groups in different cities, or to hearten solitary families seeking comradeship. Thus Molly Walsh has started in the English *Catholic Worker* a Family Forum for the exchange of ideas and experiences. Her own story is the very unusual one of a family growing up inside what may be called a larger family—for she and her husband lived the first years of married life

in a House of Hospitality which they had established
in a large poverty-stricken area. The first issue of the
Forum dealt with family holidays for poorer wage-
earners. This is a matter that greatly concerns French
Catholics also. Abbé Godin's brother has now organized
two large houses to take care of working families on
vacation. But so far the English movement is smaller
and more personal. Mrs. Walsh tells of farms where a
family can stay cheaply and of united groups at the
seaside. A letter in the next issue gave another answer
furnished by one family—and not a rich family either:

I was very interested in your article on holidays where you
said "the normal seaside holidays are beyond the reach of a
large number of people, especially those with more than two
children." For years our family have realized this, and have
saved up and bought a coach caravan to give families with
children a holiday at a reasonable price.

We now need a seaside site for it near a Catholic Church
in the North West. I wonder if any of your readers could help
us in this matter?

Housing restrictions in England, added to the frightful
shortage brought about by the blitz and the cessation
of building during the war, have produced the curious
phenomenon of a positive rash of caravans all over the
country and large quantities of boats used as dwellings
on most of the rivers. Too small to solve satisfactorily the
family housing problem, they could certainly help us
in meeting that of cheap holidays.

But many other questions are raised in this Forum,
and much of the second issue is so important that I quote
it at length:

"I don't think people realize just how tough the going not
only can be, but very often is, to bring up a family in a big

c

town. And it is no wonder that many people give up the struggle to live up to the Church's teaching. When I was married in the middle of the war, I thought we'd only have to rough it for a bit and then things would become more normal, but it gets more difficult every year. We have four children now and are still in the same three rooms.

"There are flats going up around us, but the rents are out of the question if you have only one low wage coming in. Several people around here have got them, but they limit themselves to only one or two children so that the wife can go out to work as well.

"My husband is still very bad with his nerves and has had to take on a lighter job. The doctor's solution was to give me a note to go to the clinic for advice—and you know what that means. Of course I have not been, but I cannot deny that I live in dread of having another baby.

"I shall have to take on extra cleaning now as the wages will be less. It is a vicious circle. It will mean that I shall have less time for the children if they are to be fed and clothed properly, and the other children around here are so very well dressed.

"Religion should help us. But it seems so remote somehow. The Young Christian Workers have done a good thing in starting something for the young lads, but unless they help the older ones to become good parents, they won't get far.

"I believe more could be done by priests personally encouraging parents, if it could be managed. I hope you don't think I'm just having a little moan to myself. I expect it would help if we were nearer the church, but away on the outskirts of the parish the priests never seem to have found us. I expect they are very busy, but you get to feel 'Doesn't anybody care what happens to us?' "

I don't think anybody could read the above letter [comments Mrs. Walsh] without some feelings on the matter, either of sympathy, fellow-feeling or just sheer frustration.

If it were a rare or isolated case, we might feel that it was none of our business. But no woman of any sensibility, who pays attention to what is going on among her neighbors in the wider sense, can fail to be aware that some part, at any rate, of this state of affairs is duplicated in at least one family or more in her immediate environment.

I think it is true to say that at present the economic factor is, generally speaking, worse in the big towns, but this is by no means the only thing which makes many women live in constant dread of having any more children.

Quite obviously God did not intend things to be like this. Our Lord gave as an example of the feelings of the deepest joy, those of a mother when her baby is born, and prophesied to an incredulous audience that the time would come when people would say "Blessed is the barren womb and blessed are the paps which have not given suck."

Nor as members of the mystical body can we shrug the problem off, so we come slap up against the question *What can I do?*

And of course no very complete answer can be given. But here are a few suggestions:

1. We can pray. We can pray for the emergence of a Christian society in which the living of a full, happy normal family life is a glory, and not, at the best, something to be accepted as a "sacrifice" and, at worst, to be evaded as far as possible. Could we not resolve to say a prayer daily for this intention? Perhaps someone will compose one for us.

2. We can examine our conscience. As I said above, the sheer economic factor is by no means the only one which makes motherhood feared. We are all, to some extent or other, infected by the entirely wrong and pagan materialist atmosphere in which we find ourselves.

We can ask ourselves seriously to what extent are our own lives governed by the material element. The desire to have many possessions, expensive furniture, costly toys for our children, even if we can have them without affecting our own family life, may be making it more difficult for someone else.

I am sure there is a definite need for all good Catholics to practice deliberately simplicity of life. When Our Lord said "Blessed are the poor in spirit," He was not speaking idly, He definitely meant that it was a happy state to be in.

Again, we can examine what I call our "sympathy of outlook." Some housewives by temperament and training can manage their homes and children very much better than others. And there is apt to be a kind of snobbery among the former class. We might ask ourselves, have we ever "sniffed" at Mrs. H.'s grubby curtains? It would be much better if we could tactfully get to know her and try to lend a helping hand.

What a difference a really sisterly feeling among women would make! If we could mind Mrs. Brown's children occasionally to give her a free afternoon. And also, I might say, if Mrs. Brown, assuming for the moment that she is the one in difficulties—perhaps temporarily, till the new baby arrives in a month or two—could accept help simply, knowing that Mrs. Smith, who is at the moment the helper, understands that you can't have the whole house spotless with three children already, and "not feeling too good for a while." Well, you can develop this theme for yourselves. I shall be glad to receive the result of your meditations in due course.

IV

Reading the letters and comments in this Family Forum, I was reminded of an incident told me by a doctor. She does much maternity work, and one day a woman came to the clinic who expected her twelfth baby. She looked a battered wreck, dragging two small children, utterly depressed, unable to face life. The doctor suddenly remembered a very beautiful baby carriage given her by a wealthy patient. It was of a type hardly ever seen today, shining with brilliant paint and chromium, hung on springs and light to push, but with seats for two children and room for parcels besides. As the woman walked away proudly pushing her two children in it, she appeared transformed: how small a thing, the doctor said, can work a change in the outlook of the very poor.

But it was more than merely the baby carriage: this gift typified the just honor shown to her condition: it expressed the com-passion of another Catholic woman: that com-passion which means suffering with, bearing the burden with, those women who have the courage today to face the fullest weight that a mother can have to bear: a large family to be brought up in a city slum.

Often that compassion appears lacking: I have heard grumbles from other worshippers against the one city church I know (the Servite Fathers, Fulham Road, London) which has a mothers' and babies' Mass. Here the small children play in the aisles. The babies sometimes cry; a beaming priest, passing to and fro, makes the mothers feel that it is all perfectly all right, that the children are in their home when they are in God's house.

Alas, I have known other churches where the priest has said from the pulpit, "Take that baby out." I have read in a parish bulletin the remark that the Sunday Mass precept is not of obligation for the mothers of children too young to be kept quiet in church. As if we went to Mass simply because it is of obligation! We *need* Mass, we *need* Communion and never more so than when babies are young, or we are carrying the unborn.

To help expectant mothers, a permit can be obtained in some English dioceses for liquid refreshment before

Communion. One of my friends had it repeatedly in one diocese; another young woman, applying in another diocese, succeeded in getting it, "But why," she asked, "did they have to make me feel like a criminal for asking for it?"

Everywhere in France relaxation of the fasting rules and evening Masses have been an immense help. In most dioceses liquid refreshment (non-alcoholic) is permitted for all communicants an hour before any Mass later than nine, while any person who has to do hard work may take liquid refreshment before setting out to church, however early the Mass may be. Communion may be received also at a midday Mass if breakfast was taken four hours earlier, while for evening Communion fasting is required from solid food for four hours, from liquid for one. These Masses are crowded, and there are many Communions.

Chesterton has truly said that the Church supremely turns towards man the merciful face of Christ. In the Gospels we sometimes witness His sternness as He denounces the hypocritical Pharisees or scourges the money changers out of the temple. But the Church shows us His Sacred Heart pierced with love for the sinner and for the poor. Mankind is mostly poor, many hearts are broken by life, and it is the boundlessness of the Saviour's compassion on which His Church insists, so that they may look up and lift up their heads to receive His salvation. But His ministers do not always show the same love and pity.

We all know in our own experience how easy it is to fail in compassion: how easy to think about our own fatigue instead of about how tired that other woman looks waiting behind us in the queue, or how tired the

bus-conductress is who has just jerked us off our feet
with her cry, "Hold very tight!" Priests too get tired,
especially when saying a midday Mass and preaching
at it. That screaming baby must rasp the nerves of a
man who has been fasting from midnight until past
midday. (The Church might perhaps in her discipline
be more compassionate with her pastors!)

But so much is said from the pulpit, so much written
in books in abuse(the word is not too strong: it might
often be qualified by the adjective "violent") of those
who are afraid of large families, frightened by all the
problems of this modern world. Could not a rather more
positive attitude be taken: things done to help heroic
mothers, things said to hearten them, pastors and
parishes more prepared to assist them? Some parish
priests are themselves heroic in their approach to the
problem: I think in particular of one in the Middle
West who gave a home for months in his presbytery to
a homeless colored family. One baby was born in this
marvellous Bethlehem.

But I have talked too with many parents who have
told me sad stories: scoldings in church for coming late
to Mass, scoldings for bringing school children with
them—"They should have gone to the children's Mass,"
help in house or garden from older children made difficult by excessive home-work and still more by school
projects (selling "chances" round the neighborhood,
getting ready for the bazaar, summoned to school on
Saturday for this or on Sunday for the other). Many
things which the parent of a solitary child may welcome
are a distress to the mother of half a dozen. It may well
be that the two eldest take a heavy burden off her
shoulders evenings and week-ends. Those are the ones

wanted for school schemes and accused of lack of school spirit if they have too much home spirit.

For the Catholic community, like the community in general, is geared to small families and needs to do quite a job of thinking if it is to embrace many large ones.

John Wu, Minister to the Vatican under Chiang Kai-shek's government, was photographed with the Holy Father sitting in the midst of his family. Someone suggested that other Ministers might be jealous, but the Pope replied that he would gladly be photographed with *any* Minister who had thirteen children.

Another advantage of the positive approach, of comforting and assisting the large family as opposed to the negative one of denouncing the small one, is that denunciation so seldom strikes the right person. Only in private and talking to an individual can one be certain of reaching the heart of his difficulty. And it may well be that what is affected by a public, and therefore generalized, denunciation is not the consciences of those who deserve it but of those to whom it certainly does not apply.

I was much distressed by the anxiety of one woman I knew whose physical condition (her Catholic doctor had spoken strongly) and whose financial condition (her husband's wage kept the existing family barely above starvation level) precluded at the moment the having of another child. The question was one of waiting a year or so. She had already three children, her husband and she were both converts and both deeply disturbed by fear of not doing right. I wrote on their behalf to one of the best theologians in England, Fr. Davis, S.J., author of *Moral and Pastoral Theology*, quoting also the saying that seems to be becoming a slogan with many apostolic families, "I want to have as many children as God sends me," and the accusation occasionally made that not to do so is to fail in trust.

Fr. Davis replied: "You will not find any reputable and responsible theologian who holds or teaches that *any* limitation of the family by self-restraint is a lack of trust in God. In fact the statement is false.

"Similarly, you will not find any theologian who holds that all families should have as many children as God sends. Of course this statement should be 'as many as God might send if parents co-operated with Him.' If this were true, most Catholic married people have been wanting in their duties since the beginning of Christianity. All along, the Church has known of small families. Yet she did not reproach them.

"Married people are not obliged to have as large families as possible biologically, and regardless of the effects on the wife's health and the maintenance of living children. The husband is seriously bound not to jeopardize the health of the wife or the decent economic condition of the family.

"A husband's duty to wife and existing children is more pressing than his obligation—if there is one—to procreate more children.

"Those people who maintain that the family should be the largest biologically possible, *coûte que coûte*, are thinking irrationally. Surely God does not wish heaven to be peopled with citizens of heaven, at the cost of duties unfulfilled by man and woman."

In a later letter Fr. Davis enclosed an extract from the Pope's allocution to the Midwives of Rome in which he states both the natural obligation of having children and the fact that circumstances may make permissible, even advisable, the limitation of the family by continence. I begin the quotation on page 8,* with the warning with which the Holy Father precedes his remarks on the abuse of "Rhythm," a warning which he follows by stating the lawfulness of its correct use (*Abusus non tollit usum*): ". . . . to embrace the married state, continuously to make use of the faculty proper to it and lawful in it alone, and, on the other hand, to withdraw always and deliberately with no serious reason from its primary obligation, would be a sin against the very meaning of conjugal life.

"There are serious motives, such as those often mentioned, in the so-called medical, eugenic, economic, and social 'indications,' that can exempt for a long time, perhaps even the whole duration of the marriage, from the positive and obligatory carrying out of the act. From this it follows that observing the non-fertile periods alone can be lawful only under a moral aspect. Under the conditions mentioned it really is so."

In a later allocution to the members of the Italian Family Front, the Holy Father returned to this subject and added that he hoped that medical researches would eventually increase the certainty of the "safe period."

To return to the allocution to the Midwives, the Holy Father continued:

Now you might observe, perhaps, that in the exercise of your profession you sometimes come across very delicate cases in which the risk of motherhood cannot be run or must be avoided completely, and in which, on the other hand, observing the sterile periods either does not give sufficient security or has to be abandoned for other reasons.

* Of the translation put out by the N.C.W.C.

And then you ask how one can still speak of an apostolate in the service of maternity.

If in your reliable and experienced judgment, conditions absolutely demand a "no," (that is that maternity must be excluded), it would be a mistake and a wrong to impose or counsel a "yes." Here we are dealing with concrete facts, with a medical not theological question, one, therefore, which you are competent to handle. But in such cases couples do not ask you for a medical answer, which is necessarily negative, but for approval of a "technique" of the conjugal act insured against the risk of motherhood. Here is another occasion on which you are called to exercise your apostolate, in so far as you do not leave any doubt that even in such extreme cases every preventive step and every direct attempt upon the life and development of the germ is in conscience prohibited and excluded, and that there is but one way open, that of complete abstinence from every complete exercise of the natural faculty. Here your apostolate obliges you to clear, sure judgment and calm firmness.

But it will be objected that such abstinence is impossible, that such heroism cannot be attained. Today you will hear and read this objection on all sides, even from those who on account of their duty and ability should be able to judge very differently. The following argument is brought forward as a proof: "No one is obliged to do the impossible and no reasonable legislator, it is assumed, wishes by his law to oblige people to do the impossible. But, for married couples long-term abstinence is impossible. Therefore they are not obliged to abstain. The Divine law cannot mean this."

Thus, from partly true premises a false conclusion is deduced. In order to convince yourself of this, invert the steps of the argument. God does not oblige people to do the impossible. But God obliges married people to abstain, if their union cannot be fulfilled according to the laws of nature. Therefore, in this case abstinence is possible. In confirmation of this argument we have the Council of Trent which, in its chapter on the observance, necessary and possible, of the commandments teaches us that, as St. Augustine said, "God does not command impossible things, but when He commands He warns us to do what can be done and to ask what cannot and gives you help so that you can" (Conc. Trid., Sess. 6, Cap. II. Denzinger n. 804, S. August. "De natura et gratia," Cap. 43, n. 50, L. Migne, vol. 44, col. 271).

Therefore, do not allow yourselves to be confused in the carrying out of your profession and your apostolate by all this talk about impossibility, either as regards your own inner judgment or in what concerns your outward conduct. Never do anything contrary to the law of God and your consciences as Christians. It is wronging men and women of our times to deem them incapable of continuous heroism. Today, for many reasons—perhaps with the goad of hard necessity or even sometimes in the service of injustice— heroism is exercised to a degree and to an extent which would have been thought impossible in days gone by. Why, then, should this heroism, if the circumstances really demand it, stop at the borders established by the passions and inclinations of nature? The answer is clear. The man who does not want to dominate himself is incapable of so doing. He who believes he can do so, counting merely on his own strength without seeking sincerely and perseveringly help from God, will remain miserably disillusioned.

One point of quite special interest emerges from this allocution. The Holy Father realistically deals with the heroism called for by abstinence from the conjugal act. It is of course true, as Fr. Vincent McNabb so frequently asserted, that to live a Christian life in any form in the crowded cities of today, more especially in the slums, calls for immense heroism. But it is perhaps too lightly assumed that the only form this heroism takes is the resolution to set no limits to the size of one's family.

There may well be immense heroism, especially on the man's side, when limitation of the family means total abstinence from intercourse over a considerable period. The joy which God has given to the expression of mutual love between husband and wife is a hard thing to forego.

And this expression has, as the Holy Father goes on to point out, a value of its own. His warning, especially, against turning the sanctuary of the home into "a mere biological laboratory" must come as something tremendously heartening to the married:

In matrimony, for the procreation of life, the Creator has destined human beings made of flesh and blood, endowed with minds and hearts: they are called as men, not animals without reason, to be the makers of their descendants. For this end God wishes that couples be united. Holy Scripture says of God that He created man to His image and that He created the human being both male and female (Gen. i, 27), that, as we find it so often in the sacred books, "man must abandon his father and his mother and unite himself with his wife forming one flesh" (Gen. ii, 24, Matt. xix, 5, Eph. v, 31).

All this, therefore, is true and so willed by God. But it must not be divorced from the primary function of marriage, which is service for new life. Not only the common work of external life but also intellectual and spiritual endowment, even the depths of spirituality in conjugal love as such, have been put by the will of nature and the Creator at the service of our descendants. By its nature, perfect married life means also the complete dedication of the parents for the benefit of their children, and in its strength and tenderness, conjugal love is itself a postulate of the most sincere care for the offspring and the guarantee of its being carried out. (St. Thomas 3, p.q. 29, a 2, in c. Supplmt. q. 49 a. 2, ad I).

To reduce cohabitation and the conjugal act to a pure

organic function for the transmission of seed would be converting the home, the sanctuary of the family, into a mere biological laboratory. In our address of September 29, 1949, to the International Congress of Catholic Doctors, We formally excluded artificial insemination from marriage. In its natural structure, the conjugal act is a personal action, a simultaneous and immediate co-operation on the part of the husband and wife which by the very nature of the agents and the propriety of the act is the expression of the mutual gift which according to Holy Scripture brings about union "in one flesh only."

This is something much more than the union of two seeds which may be brought about even artificially, without the natural action of husband and wife. The conjugal act, ordained and willed by nature, is a personal act of co-operation, the right to which husband and wife give each other when they marry.

One lesson that emerges from the words of the Holy Father is a reminder of the old ideal of individual vocation. "See that thou make it in all things," God told Moses, "according to the pattern showed thee on the mount." The material for the building is the very circumstances of a man's or a woman's life. But the pattern, though it may and should become visible to each one on the mount of prayer, may also be clouded by each one's own desires, self-will and feelings. Hence the value of direction.

And here, I think, Abbé Godin has given us a discovery of immense value. It is almost essential that a couple seeking guidance should go to the same director.

There used to be in our family a standing joke about certain old ladies who loved to talk of "my director." How curious (we said) that he always gave each one the direction she would have given to herself. Old

ladies are not the only people whose subconscious selves
send up a problem so stated that only one answer is
possible. A wife whose (Catholic) doctor had urged that
she must for her health's sake let a year pass before
another child was heard of found her confessor in complete agreement. But her husband making a retreat was
told a week later that they should trust God "heroically"
and go right ahead!

Even close friends may know nothing of the intimate
struggles revealed to the confessor, and surely for them
there is only one course—an effort at ever deepening
charity and compassion.

Parents of large families describe how they have
suffered when neighbors shrugged scornfully on finding
that a seventh child was on the way. Yet they too often
show their own condemnation of the small family and
take for granted that greed for mink coats or new cars
is the underlying cause. Can they not rather try to
believe that there may be some very good reason which
they happen not to know? Ill health and, still more,
extreme poverty are often carefully concealed. And there
are also parents who married too late or are physically
unable to have a large family.

I suppose, however, that any enthusiastic group living
together, inspiring and emulating one another, tends to
lose sense of proportion and to use exaggerated language.
Thus did some of the early hermits talk, as though salvation were only to be found in the desert. Thus did Saint
Bernard's youthful monks talk as though their brothers
who contemplated matrimony must be snatched as
brands from the burning! A friend of mine, speaking of
a young priest who was advocating families of a dozen,
said, "I can bear it much better when the parents talk

that way. I'd like to ask him if he stays in the confessional as long as the Curé d'Ars."

One argument in particular is brought by those who protest vehemently against the avoidance of "too many" children, even through the exercise of complete continence. How do we know, they ask, which is too many? Fr. Vincent McNabb was an eleventh, Saint Catherine of Siena a twenty-fifth child. Who are we to refuse life to a possible saint?

Carry this argument to its logical conclusion and you would have to say that nobody at all must remain unmarried. I certainly have known people who seem (apart from the higher dedication of religious vows) to hold precisely this view. But it is clearly not the common teaching of the Church. Long engagements are the usual practice in Ireland for people who "cannot afford" to marry young—and this is only another way of refusing to have a large family. The responsibility of choosing, which lies upon all men, is a real and a serious responsibility. Prayer is needed and good hard thought—but it remains our responsibility.

(As for Saint Catherine, her mother lived to a hearty old age—and the family were so well-to-do that they adopted a twenty-sixth child!)

A certain confusion of thought appears to underly the remark already referred to with which many magnificent parents "simplify" the problem. "We intend to have as many children as God sends us. Not to do so is to fail to trust God." The confusion lies in the omission of secondary causes, the inference that the matter of having children has been placed by God altogether outside His usual pattern for human living.

"The heaven of heavens is the Lord's, the earth He hath given to the children of men."

Christopher Dawson tells us that, of old, men were so much aware of the earth as God's gift that they viewed the tilling of it "as a religious rite by which they co-operated as priests and hierophants in the great cosmic mystery of the fertilization and growth of nature. . . . There was a profound sense that man lived not by his own strength and knowledge, but by his acting in harmony with the divine cosmic powers."

How far better was this imperfect natural religion than the religion of money and the machine, that has led to the earth's rape, the destruction of its fertility. Christianity, too, calls us a priestly people—in a higher sense indeed but in one that includes all that the primitive religions vaguely suggested. Man is a priest when he co-operates with God in creating food, far more when he co-operates with God in the birth of a child. But in either case, God has left to man a free choice.

"The earth He has given to the children of men." And so man must plough, harrow and sow the seed: when he has done this "the earth of itself brings forth fruit, first the blade, then the ear and then the full corn in the ear." In a year when he has left a field unsown the farmer does not expect God to send a crop. Man is secondary cause, is co-creator with God, of that loaf of bread—and also of that baby. If he does everything to produce a baby, he is *not* simply having the child God chooses to send—he is having the child he took all human means to have.

Thus in India we have the spectacle of vast multitudes of babies born only to die in a nation-wide famine. "More

D

souls for heaven," says one type of idealistic Catholic quite happily. But it is not really as simple as that. God has made us citizens of earth also, has given us the task of building the earthly city as well as of preparing for the heavenly.° And it is not the *true* ideal that parents should bring into the world a little skeleton covered with sores and marked for death, thereby making the earning of a livelihood for themselves and their other children even more impossible.

I have taken an extreme case, for even in the most extreme, it is with, and not contrary to, nature that man must act if he is to obey the God of nature.

Yet it is true, too, that at the other end of the scale we have the horrifying spectacle of people who really do prefer the automobile to the baby or who choose for one child an expensive school and therefore deny to a second or third the gift of life.

For all this a great weight of responsibility lies upon us all. We are "members one of another" in Christ's Mystical Body, and the physical sufferings on the one side, the false mental attitudes on the other, should affect us as truly as a sore hand or a broken leg affects the whole body. Where we can we must help materially. Where we can we must help spiritually.

And the last is the more important. The only real remedy for fear of life is love of life, the only real remedy for sterility is vitality. When men love life they are eager to pass it on. Death is one remedy for disease, but health is another.

It is strange how one pattern can be glimpsed underneath all creation, animate and inanimate, God's pat-

° See above Fr. Davis (pp. 25-6), and the Holy Father (passage in italics, p. 26 *et seq*).

tern of vitality, and how man in this age has overlaid it
with a pattern of death. Dust bowls, deforestation, steri-
lization, artificial birth control, legalized abortion, euthanasia: even those who defend one or other of these
things must admit that all are against one thing—all are
against life.

The mention of euthanasia calls to mind a further
problem of the Catholic family today, which is fast
becoming an enormous one. We may decide whether
or when to have another child, we cannot decide whether
to have old parents, aunts, uncles, grandparents. And
I solemnly believe that the day is at hand when "advice
from the clinic" will take us beyond the killing of the
unborn to the killing of the old and bedridden. The days
are gone when large houses and cheap labor made a
patriarchal style of living easy for many, when unemployed wives and sisters made it possible for almost all.
Old people need care. They cannot live alone, least of
all within the slender limits of an old age pension. All
the Homes for the Aged are filled to bursting point, they
usually have long waiting lists. And, anyhow, can this
be the ideal? Visit any old man or women in the best of
these places and you find they are craving for their own
children, their one desire is really to "go home."

I was talking lately to a nun who does the visiting for
a large London parish. I asked her whether she needed
any help for the poorer families she visited. She answered, "The families are fairly well situated. Most of
them are getting good money and they all have one
another. The great problem of the parish is the lonely
old people."

I wonder how many readers of this book possess as a
part of their household elderly relatives who have to be

taken care of. In my experience, very many Catholic families even today are made up of three generations— a thing rather uncommon outside Catholic circles.

There is one family I know in New York, a fairly young couple who have been married ten years and have five children. The two smallest sleep with their parents, the older boys in bunk beds in a very small room. A settee in the living room serves for the grandmother while the great-grandfather and an uncle sleep in the only remaining bedroom. It would be quite impossible for them all to take a meal simultaneously in the small dining room-kitchen. This family are hoping to build themselves a house and get into the country before very long. Meanwhile, let them serve as typical in thinking of this part of the family problem today. If the housing situation makes it difficult to have and to bring up a large family of children, what does it do to the situation of the old?

I have been filled with admiration of my New York friends, and of families that I know in England, as they cheerfully tackle the daily problems in an atmosphere of astonishing serenity. Out of three old people one is almost certain to be in bed with some ailment. Then, too, the moment arrives with each one when it is not safe to leave him or her alone with the children, when making tea may very well lead to scalds or burns, and when it becomes indispensable to take time out every day for the individual care of each one of them.

There is, of course, another side to the picture. To the Catholic, who not only accepts the commandment to honor his parents but who is also deeply aware of the debt of gratitude he owes them, there is a profound delight in being able to come to their assistance. Nevertheless, the burden may be a heavy one even for people reasonably well housed. For those who lack space it is almost and sometimes quite impossible. There must today be old people whose families literally cannot take care of them. There are others who have no families.

Again, surely the responsibility is not that of the individual family alone, but of all the families that together make up the Church, Christ's body. If one member suffer or rejoice, the rest suffer and rejoice with it. Christian love beginning with and from the family must find a way to rebuild that community life we once had and have now lost.

One effort being made in this direction spontaneously and simultaneously in many countries—in Italy, for instance, in Ireland, England, Canada and the United States—is the grouping of families into associations for the building of their own houses. The ordinary house today is too small for a normal Catholic family, especially when complete with old people as well as children. A much larger house can be built by people for themselves much cheaper than bought; and comradeship, first in building together, later in living together, results in a pattern of Christian co-operation widely different from that of other communities in the world today.

Of these communities one called Marycrest is referred to below by Ed Willock and is within half an hour's drive from the George Washington Bridge, New York City.

Fourteen families are engaged in the scheme: they all help in the building and they give priority to the family whose needs are most urgent. Four families are now settled on the sixty-three-acre site, each having a one-acre homestead, the rest of the land being held in common. A road had to be made, trees to be felled. All the settlers are dependent on a weekly wage, and the down-payments on material have come as loans from friends who realize the value of the scheme. Week-ends and holidays see groups of men arriving from New York and the walls of a fresh house gradually rising, through hard and gruelling work. Those already on the spot lend constant help, complete their own dwellings and develop their gardens. Frequent meetings, sometimes of men only, sometimes of the entire community, keep them in step from a practical viewpoint and stir up their enthusiasm for the ideals of freedom and the family on which the movement is based.

There is a new closeness of fellowship. "I can ask Alan or Jack," said one, "for a loan or to come and help in the house or garden, where I would hesitate to ask my own brother." And another of them compared this grouping of families to the closeness with one's own wife and children. Like the Walshes in the English Catholic Worker Movement, but even more completely, these people feel they have two families.

"It seems almost absurd," Christopher Dawson once wrote, "to expect people to bring the spirit of Galilee and Assisi into the environment of Hollywood and Chicago. No Christian can deny that it is possible. But it involves something more than pious platitudes and ethical idealism. It calls for a heroic effort like that which converted the Roman Empire. . . . It is not enough for us to sit still and wait for an apocalyptic solution of our problems. The saint, like every other great man, is the organ of a social purpose, and the success of his mission depends on the reserves of faith and spiritual will that have been accumulated by the anonymous activity of ordinary imperfect men and women, each of whom has made an individual contribution, however minute it may be, to a new order of Christian life."

All sociology, Fr. Vincent McNabb used to say, should begin from the Gospels: this remarkable formula appears all the more striking when we study its application in such a country as the United States. Because the States are so immensely rich and so far advanced in all the applied sciences, the idea has grown up in Europe, and especially in France, that they are more materialistic than other countries. No one looking impartially at France and at the States feels much inclined to concede this. French materialists (of whom there are many) are every bit as materialistic as American materialists. And American idealists (of whom there are also many) are perhaps the most complete idealists in the world today. For when he gives up his materialism the American has more to give up of goods and of opportunity—and he gives up, as he gives, lavishly and wholeheartedly.

The cult of poverty, to be seen in so many of our stories, is one example of this new and generous American sociology, the cult of the family is another. Next comes the abandonment, when possible, of urban civilization, the constant search for the great ideas and ideals of Christianity in the Bible and in the Christian Classics, the increasing effort to base all life on trust in God's Providence.

There is also in the best Catholic thinking of America today a searching and determined self-criticism. In an article in *Integrity* Marion Stancioff quoted a "displaced" European priest as astonishing her by saying that not enough was done for youth in America. He went on to explain his meaning: youth is a time of generous enthu-

siasm, and the modern world gives it no proper food.
Children are told of red Indians and cowboys. Their
love of courage is often misdirected towards gangsters.
They are brought from a world of fantasy into a world
where business is business—their highest possibilities
totally undeveloped.

Ideally, Christianity as such should correct this edu-
cational evil: in practice it does not always do so. But
such groupings of Christian families as Marycrest furnish
an answer in a twofold way. They give a practical answer, because the children are able to help in house and
garden, to develop skills uncalled for in the city, to
share the lives of parents who themselves are fully human
beings with all sides of them developed and masters of
a multitude of skills.

They give an ideal answer because they develop
ideals: these families are truly neighbors. Who, asked
Our Lord, was neighbor to the man who fell among
thieves? He who showed mercy to him. Go thou and do
in like manner. Daily in all lives come chances to be a
neighbor, but in these small communities a very wilful
blindness would be needed to neglect them. Then, too,
nobler heroes than the cowboy or the gangster are proposed to the imitation of youth. Life is not soft at Marycrest, and the lives of the saints do not appear too unreal
and distant.

In this same article Marion Stancioff tells of how a non-
Christian friend of hers took his children to Rome to
inspire them with the great examples of ancient heroism,
of how in some lands Communist youth have trained
themselves to undergo torture voluntarily, so as to grow
strong in courage and be in no danger of betraying their
friends should they be later put to this fearful test. The

article is called "Reluctant Heroes," and it strikes the
same note as the Holy Father when he writes of the
heroism often shown for evil causes in the age we are
living in. It is a time, he says, of heroism as well as a
time of fearful suffering. And there are in all human
beings, especially the young, deep reserves of heroism,
did we but dare to call them forth.

It is often said that we are today witnessing the end
of an age, not unlike the breaking-up of the Roman
Empire; it is also said that we are at the beginning of a
New Age. The end of the Roman Empire was merged
in the beginning of the Christian Church. To us who are
Christians it seems evident that the same Church, the
same Christ, who makes all things new, is giving us a
chance today to restore all things in Him once more.

And as we think in terms of Jane who must sleep with
her grandmother, or Bill who is nearly dead trying to
build a house for his mother and aunt and wife and five
children, we hear the echoes of all these personal problems reverberating in the mighty echoes of world history.
This is how the great historian of Western man, Christopher Dawson, has described our plight today and pointed
to an issue in which the Christian past guides us towards
a Christian future.

"Western civilization today is threatened with the loss
of its freedom and its humanity. It is in danger of substituting dead mechanism for living culture. Hedonism
cannot help, nor yet rationalism. It can be saved only by
a renewal of life. And this is impossible without love,
for love is the source of life, both physically and spiritually. . . .

"Hence the restoration of the religious view of marriage which is the Catholic ideal is the most important

of all the conditions for a solution of our present difficulties. Its importance cannot be measured by practical
considerations, for it means the re-introduction of a
spiritual principle into the vital centre of human life."*

V

This book would be called in France *Temoignages*.
For the French specialize in books in which the gathered
experiences of many are brought together in rich illu-
mination of some single theme. The theme of this book
is God's Providence in relation to Catholic families who
put their trust in Him.

A very old and holy friend of mine once told me that
she sometimes became almost physically aware of the
great ocean of divine grace surrounding us, which would
come flooding into our souls if we did but open them
wider. These stories and many others I have been told
bring this home more than any single experience, even
one far more individually tremendous. For here we see a
multitude of lives all lovingly and personally guided by
God, sometimes through sorrow, sometimes through joy.

The stories are in one aspect amazingly varied, rang-
ing from a refugee family, that barely escaped destruction between the Nazis and the Communists, to peaceful
Americans living a home life on a family farm; from
people with twelve children to those who sorrowed that
a family was denied them, or bore the cross of a mentally deficient son. Yet in another aspect they seem
amazingly alike: one pattern runs through them, the
pattern which humanity had always known, but of which
it only learned the name after Christ had sanctified it—
the pattern of the Cross. Each one has his own special

* *Enquiries into Religion and Culture*, p. 291.

cross, made to his shape, hurting where he needs the hurt, bearing more lightly where he needs relief, but no life is without it.

And one element all have in common, and all these stories repeat it: it is *just,* and only just, before breaking-point is reached, that God comes to the rescue, sometimes almost visibly. On the strongest and most courageous He seems to put a burden that the rest of us could never carry, but He allows everyone to realize that he could not carry alone even the lighter burden that is his. Some of our stories are almost dramatic in their tales of help that came well past the eleventh hour—the money that bought a house or saved a farm, the transportation that arrived *just* before the Russians did, food brought in quantities to a family the very evening the parents had given their last coins to rescue another family from a hungry night on a park bench. Others tell rather of the steady working of providential guidance over the years, others mainly of that internal gift of the Holy Spirit whereby the heaviest of crosses becomes at last bearable. But they all, I think without exception, strike the note that God will test us by delay, that we constantly fail in the trust that should surely have become a habit after the number of times that the needed help has come. "Help always came in time," says D. H.; and Bill Walsh moralizes over his own breakdown into "a sort of rage of pain in which the providence of God is accused of cruel delay." His wife reminds him that help has always come and adds, "*in time* means that help will come before it is actually too late, not just before it is too late for comfort." And Bill agrees, thinking of Christ in the Garden, "Actually it *is* His mercy that makes help come too late. He allows us to suffer with Him."

The individual character of the cross marks the fact that each soul has its own vocation. If we did not realize this fact, nothing would be more puzzling than the different behavior patterns of different people. If we did realize this fact, we should be slower in our judgments of others. To take one small instance: the author of one of the stories tells how she and her husband decided for the sake of their other children to leave their mentally deficient son in a children's Home. I have known two other families where they told me they had kept such a child with them, and that his brothers and sisters had learnt gentleness and consideration from living with him. Yet if these were right, need the others have been wrong? The relative age of the children, the size of the house, the quality of the care available, all these considerations can modify or wholly change a situation.

And again, while one man might feel obliged to give up his dreams of creative and artistic work, or of life on the land, and support his family by a clerical job he loathes, another might judge (with the same strong desire to do right) that he should risk a smaller salary or an uncertain career for the sake of their physical and spiritual health and of his own.

The same thing applies, as I have said above, to the question of the size of a family. As long as we are quite clear on the Church's teaching in the matter, we can joyfully and with fullest admiration read the story of those heroic people who have responded to what in their case was doubtless God's call to a reckless trust and acceptance of an enormous family. I have put in two of these stories, only regretting in one of them a slight tendency to throw stones in the general direction of fellow-Catholics who may well be guided by God in a path of continence, no less heroic.

One aspect must be emphasized in stories of God's providence. His guidance and care of us are shown every bit as much in day-to-day life as in those sudden happenings which make the best material for a story. While God's little miracles are often scattered among his children, it remains true that he helps those who help—not themselves so much as their families. It has been said to me that some stories of providential help suggest substituting for a good day's work reliance on God and on your neighbor. If you just sit and fold your hands, a check will come in the post from someone else who has been working to earn it.

This would indeed be a distorted view, and, in fallen human nature every virtue does carry the danger of a corresponding vice. Hard workers may forget the one thing necessary; contemplatives may forget the duty of work. Those who tend to live unreflectively from day to day may mistake natural recklessness for supernatural trust. I remember the slightly wry remark of a very fine woman: "I'm the worldly one, so I suppose I shall have to educate all my sister's children."

No, we do not even know which are the "worldly" ones, or whether a family that just "cannot get on" is held back by lack of energy or by a true vocation to poverty. God tells them, but He does not tell us. And each one has to discover for himself with earnest prayer whether he is answering God's call or simply that of his own inclinations.

What I have seen of the families in this book reveals an alarming level of hard and gruelling toil, and also a wealth of spiritual experience that is continually growing.

A phrase in Nancy Du Bois' story especially struck me: "In conclusion—but actually what conclusion can

there be, since this is life going on, day by day, for
a man and his wife and his children?" These stories
do seem to me extraordinarily vital. At moments I
have wanted to take the pen out of the writers' hands
when I felt they were not doing justice to the splendor
of their own lives. Yet it is far better that each should
tell his own story from inside. I would have liked to say
something of what I saw in Vermont of the students
surrounding Paul and Susan Zens, getting from them
such amazing stores of spiritual help, filling the house
with the gaiety and warmth of a family almost as real as
the one they had longed for, perhaps even greater in
its power for good. I would have liked to write of the
DuBois' life on their little farm, of Donald's pleasure in
his tractor and Nancy's in her house, of their Roadside
Stand with its grapes and tomatoes, of the boys growing
up in the healthy country air. I must say one word of
what this family has meant for me, for I was one of those
well-meaning but most mistaken friends to whom Nancy
refers, who doubted the wisdom of her marriage. I
accepted the dictum of people who knew more than I
did about interracial matters, that it would set back the
movement fifty years. We were wrong. This marriage, so
very specially happy and well-adjusted, I now believe
has done as much as fifty years' work could do to *advance*
the movement. I rejoice in this opportunity of making
it more widely known.

Another rather unusual story, that of Bob and Molly
Walsh, I have also seen at close quarters, and I think it
has for us all most valuable lessons on the high degree
of integration possible between the family and the
apostolate. Especially in these days when the widest and
best of all apostolates is that of the family, and not of

one family alone, but of families grouped in fruitful unity, a microcosm of the living Church and its representative in a given locality.

The story of Marycrest which I have touched on in this introduction is mixed in with that of the Willocks, told so admirably by Ed. And here, as with all the other stories, "this is life going on day by day," often a hard and hurting life. Since Ed wrote "Marriage for Keeps" he has been very ill, life has been very hard for them both; but Dorothy added, "We are living examples of God's providence," for assistance has come at every step to help them in carrying the heavy cross of sickness and its result. These two do not feel that God is providing any the less, when He sends them the cross, than when He sends consolation.

All the stories in this book are stories of Christian hope as well as of faith and charity. And of all the virtues, the modern world has most completely lost hope.

The modern man has a cult of despair. If you tell him that the stories of God's help that came suddenly are all true, he will lift his eyebrows cynically and recount all the tragedies and disasters overwhelming in a tidal flood countries as well as families. How then can it be maintained that the God who lets these things happen is interested in a home for the Rogans or in health for Ed Willock?

Hope as a theological virtue, hope anchored on the world to come, appears to him quite absurd—a mere get-out used by the Catholic when earthly hopes are dim. And indeed hope, we can agree, is not an easy virtue, especially if it is not upheld by high faith and glowing charity.

But in the midst of the burning flames of modern life

the Christian family stands, like the three young men
in the fiery furnace. "Now if you be ready," says the
world, "when you hear the sound of sackbut and psaltery
and all kinds of music fall down and worship my statue."
And like Sidrach, Misach, and Abdenago the family
answers, "We know that God is able to deliver us. But if
He will not, be it known unto you that we will not worship your golden statue." The paradox of Christianity lies
in a hope set beyond this world which yet is ever conscious of present help here and now, never forgetting
that the hairs of our head are numbered and that we are
of far more value than the birds or the flowers which yet
God loves and cherishes.

A visit to one or other of the families whose stories are
told here leads the mind into fields of speculation about
this Providence which sometimes looks so odd. With
some of these thoughts I will end this rather rambling
introduction to our stories.

After Man's first disobedience, the sentence of God
combined punishment and blessing: Man was to create
his bread through sweat and toil—but through sweat and
toil the bread would be there. Woman was to bear children in pain and labor—but the children would rejoice
her. Eve said, "I have gotten a man from the Lord."

The power to pro-create, the co-creation with God of
the fruits of nature—all this mankind was still to keep—
albeit through toil and sorrow.

Our Lord came, He said, "not to destroy but to fulfil."
Yet it may well be that the Apostles when they saw Him
multiplying bread and fish, when they heard Him say,
"Be not solicitous . . . for your heavenly Father hath care
of you," thought for an instant that the age-long law of

labor had passed away and a millennium come for them in which they need toil no more. If so, how puzzled they must have been at the command to gather up the fragments that nothing should be lost: at the orders given by Our Lord to make all preparations for the Last Supper, at the question concerning the results of their fishing after the Resurrection.

But probably they made no such mistake: there has never been even a heretical group who thought of these gifts of Christ's as more than a heavenly half-holiday vouchsafed to human toilers. God still does give these holidays, these treats, just as He did in His life upon earth. Such a story as "Babies, Bills and Mr. Blue" shows Him doing it. But man must still labor, he must procreate, must build his home, grow his bread, combine with others in a fellowship of work and of worship.

Those words, "Be not solicitous," had in them a profounder meaning for generations yet to come. Chesterton was not the first person to discover that there are paradoxes in Christianity. We are to be at peace in the midst of warfare, at rest in the midst of labor, "Needy yet enriching many, having nothing yet possessing all things."

The Saints have exemplified in every age the two sides of this Christian view of life: none has toiled as they have, but they have known that God alone could give the increase. The Saints, especially of active charity, amaze us, not least those of recent years. St. John Bosco multiplying the rolls for the breakfast of his hundred boys, the Curé d'Ars miraculously filling the granary with wheat, St. Joseph Cottolengo giving away anything left over in the evening, because his vast family lived under the sign of God's Providence and must depend wholly

E

upon it day by day—"Take no thought for the morrow . . ."

But matter of special interest in the modern world is the degree to which the Christian family is aspiring to share both in the total trust and the practice of the counsels of perfection that for many generations were thought to be the prerogative of the monk and nun alone. The spirituality of the laity, the layman's—and more especially the family's—method of sanctifying and embracing poverty—these are topics today of frequent discussion and consideration.

In the history of the Church the spear-head of Christian effort has varied with the ages. At the beginning the tiny Christian community seems to act as one whole. But presently the martyrs stand out, then later it is the hermits who flock in their thousands into the desert. Presently the monks are tilling the wilderness and gathering around them the Christian people. Next come the great missionaries, so that a man like Saint Patrick is the creator of a new Christian nation—and that one of the greatest the world has ever known. Later, when faith and love need a fresh awakening, the Franciscan message, especially of love, the Dominican message, especially of truth, are brought by the friars.

In this last age of ours it would seem that the central place in penetrating modern paganism is held by the family. They are the chief Christian heroes of today and the stories in this book show us a little of the greatness of their heroism.

You remember how Saint Theresa of Avila spoke one day to God. "No wonder you have so few friends, Lord, considering the way you treat them." The reward of trust often appears to be trial. If some of our stories tell of God's treats for His children, others tell of that "chastisement whereof all are made partakers" (Heb. xii, 8), "for what son is there whom the father doth not correct?" (v.7). "Now all chastisement for the present indeed seemeth not to bring with it joy, but sorrow: but afterwards it will yield to those that are exercised by it the most peaceable fruit of justice (v.11)."

A retreat master once said, "Christianity does not take away from us the burden of life, but it gives us a spirit to bear that burden." And no one looking back over a long life can fail to see in things hard to bear, in prayers that seemed unanswered, the very material out of which peace and happiness were later built. "Your sorrow shall be turned into joy," Our Lord said to the Apostles before His Passion—not simply followed by joy but *turned into* it. And sometimes we receive that joy here and now.

Trust in God is often put to a hard test. It will not survive unless our hopes are set higher than this world sets hope. Saint Paul (or it may be a disciple full of his spirit) has given us in the Epistle to the Hebrews the picture of today reflected in the mirror of the past.

That whole glorious epistle should be studied, but it is the last three chapters that seem especially meant to help us in a meditation upon the world of today as a Catholic must see it. Against the vast background of eternity he sets the sufferings of the chosen people and God's miraculous support in those sufferings—and then in the foreground comes the Christian life of every day as the little community is living it.

"Now Faith," Chapter eleven begins, "is the substance of things to be hoped for, the evidence of things that appear not. . . .

"By faith we understand that the world was framed by the word of God; that from invisible things visible things might be made (v.3)."

In this faith we are shown the picture of the patriarchs living from age to age, Noe building the ark, Abraham leaving his country, "for he looked for a city that hath foundations whose builder and maker is God."

Isaac, Jacob, Sara all hold to God's promises, "confessing that they are strangers and pilgrims on earth"; Joseph prophesies the departure from Egypt, Moses leaves it in faith. By faith God's people passed the Red Sea, by faith the walls of Jericho fell down.

"And what shall I yet say? For the time would fail me to tell of Gedeon, Barac, Samson, Jephthe, David, Samuel, and the prophets:

"Who by faith conquered kingdoms, wrought justice, obtained promises, stopped the mouth of lions.

"Quenched the violence of fire, escaped the edge of the sword, recovered strength from weakness, became valiant in battle, put to flight the armies of foreigners.

"Women received their dead raised to life again. But others were racked, not accepting deliverance, that they might find a better resurrection.

"And others had trial of mockeries and stripes: moreover also of bands and prisons.

"They were stoned, they were cut asunder, they were tempted, they were put to death by the sword, they wandered about in sheepskins, in goatskins, being in want, distressed, afflicted:

"Of whom the world was not worthy: wandering in deserts, in mountains and in dens and in caves of the earth" (Vv. 32–8).

"And therefore we also having so great a cloud of

witnesses over our head, laying aside every weight and
sin which surrounds us, let us run by patience to the
fight proposed to us:

"Looking on Jesus, the author and finisher of faith,
who, having joy set before him, endured the cross,
despising the shame, and now sitteth on the right hand
of the throne of God. . .

"For you are not come to a mountain that might be
touched and a burning fire and a whirlwind and darkness and storm . . .

"But you are come to Mount Sion and to the city of
the living God, the heavenly Jerusalem, and to the
company of many thousands of angels.

"And to the church of the firstborn who are written
in the heavens, and to God the judge of all, and to the
spirits of the just made perfect.

"And to Jesus the mediator of the new testament, and
to the sprinkling of blood which speaketh better than
that of Abel. . . .

"Therefore, receiving an immovable kingdom, we have
grace: whereby let us serve, pleasing God, with fear
and reverence.

"For our God is a consuming fire."

After these terrific words (you really should read the
whole thing), we turn breathless to the last chapter,
in which the moral which is the model for our daily
lives is drawn, and we are startled in an opposite way.
Is this an anti-climax to the sufferings? How can this
merit the high promises?

"Let the charity of the brotherhood abide in you.

"And hospitality do not forget: for by this some, being
not aware of it, have entertained angels.

"Remember them that are in bands, as if you were

bound with them: and them that labour, as being yourselves also in the body.

"Marriage honourable in all, and the bed undefiled. For fornicators and adulterers God will judge.

"Let your manners be without covetousness, contented with such things as you have. For he hath said: *I will not leave thee: neither will I forsake thee.*"

Yes, it is all there. Around us are people who have been tortured in prisons, women who have received their dead again, others who will never again know their families but who are living in faith awaiting "a country that has foundations." And Saint Paul tells us that we belong to the same community, that if we do not have to suffer such things, "do not forget to do good and impart; for by such sacrifices God's favour is obtained."

The mystery of human life links up with the Gospel paradoxes: the Gospel is the key to the lock of that mystery. We must believe when all looks hopeless, we must work because God works for us. Again and again a flash of something that looks miraculous will shine through the clouds that cover the divine presence in our midst. But oftenest, as our stories show, God will make use of secondary causes. And if one man is not neighbor to the wounded by the wayside, God will have to find another neighbor for him. For so humanity is divinely constituted: " Do not forget to do good and to impart."

PART TWO

Families

BABIES, BILLS AND MR. BLUE

WILLIAM GAUCHAT

AT THE TIME, we were "romantic agrarians" in the worst sense of Doctor Furfey's acid epithet.

If we were smart commercial farmers, I mean to say, we could count on the government to send us a check. I don't know what for, but then neither does the government. I think of old Meilander, down the road; he gets checks, the kind of stiff cardboard ones you can't fold, wrinkle or bend, every month. And for the life of him, he says, he can't figure out for what. But he cashes them just the same.

We're poor folks—it seems funny to say that because we don't feel that way at all. We're happy as old Ned—whoever he is—but anyway we are happy. That is we were until the mail came one morning. The bank sent a notice, rather nasty too, with a note of finality about it. We were only three months back in our payments. We had written them explaining about my recent misfortune, but evidently they weren't interested in my broken bones.

"What'll we do?" asks Dot.

"Stick it in *Mr. Blue*," says I, referring to the letter. I had a full morning's work ahead of me getting the Fordson started.

A Fordson tractor is a wonderful tool. Or it was thirty years ago. It has power, noise and push when once it runs. We bought ours for fifty dollars—ten dollars down and five dollars a month. Somehow, it didn't seem right to spend money for repairs when we had not entirely paid for it. (Being romantic agrarians it was "agin" our principles to have a tractor, but a team of horses would cost two hundred dollars and the Fordson was only fifty with the plows.)

I guess we are romantic. We feel it's a good deal more attractive than being a couple of practical Social Security numbers. We're awfully in love. And we sure love "agrarianism." We love it for the same reason that the millions of urbanites do who jam rural highways with limousines, convertibles, and jalopies every Sunday afternoon from April to November: for fresh air, for the sight of a wood beyond a field of grain; for the thrill of seeing the first sticky little leaves, or blossoms whitening an orchard in May; for the blessed breeze that comes and goes all summer while city streets reflect malodorous waves of heat. I say, we love it, as does the Sunday tourist, for the sight of skies unblurred by smoke and fumes, the view of far horizons. We love it, moreover, for the apple on our bough, free for the picking, free from the merchandising, the trucking, and fifteen handlings; the fuel in our woodlot clean and free of the weight of corporation profits, starvation wages, transportation costs, bottle-necks, profit-necks, middlemen, or any evil or unnecessary thing whatever. It gives heat as we cut it and heat as we burn it. You get to love the apple as it grows and the wood as you cut it.

There is the blessed freedom of working as a man, freely spending knowledge, skill, and strength upon soil

and plant and animal and fowl, and freely taking the
benefits from sun and rain and seasons and the precious
earth. The feeling comes that "God is more intimate
here!" There is the dropping into bed dog-tired but
cheered at the thought of tomorrow's work. . . .

Then too there is our country pastor. The first time I
met him he was hoeing his garden. In dungarees, and
white shirt open at the neck and quite damp at the back,
he beamed at me through slightly steamed bi-focals. I
complimented him sincerely on his garden. It was large,
lush, weedless. "It is the blessings I give it from the
Rituale," he explained. "Of course, the truckload of
manure Joey Degan brings me every spring and fall does
help a little." The happy gleam that came through·the
steamed spectacles was like the sun breaking through an
overcast. Then he showed me his chickens, and three
goats, after which he wrote down my name and gave me
a box of envelopes.

We love this living in the country from the first lilac
bud in February and the bright green spears of wild
garlic piercing the fallen, dead leaves in the woods (and
that's when we get our new batch of chicks) to the
full moon in January on a world of whiteness cold as
fifteen below zero (one year). (We had to put the
children in bed with us that night so we all would keep
warm.)

"City farmers" the old-time farmers call us. And that
used to hurt. Until we parsed the phrase out neatly—we
were now farmers who came from the city. That was true.
These old-timers have hearts of gold (kind of encrusted
by old mother earth though).

It was a good day—the Fordson started without very
much trouble and I got a half-dozen lands plowed before

lunch. During this splendid sacramental, Dot asks about the letter from the bank. "They sounded serious."

"They always do."

"But this was a sort of super-serious one."

"You think they mean business?" (An idiotic, I mean, idiomatic phrase that means, it seems, that someone is going to get hurt.)

"Definitely."

"Where's the letter now?"

"In *Mr. Blue* and he's bulging," says she.

We always put our bills and extra money (when we have it) in *Mr. Blue*. It sounded ominous that he was bulging. That could only mean that the bills were piling up on us. It was so long ago that we put cash in *Mr. Blue*.

I suppose it sounds odd. Why we picked on *Mr. Blue* as a depositary, out of all the volumes that filled our bookshelves, I can't imagine except that we loved him so much.

When we were single and simple we used to judge people by *Mr. Blue*.* If you loved *Mr. Blue* we loved you; you "belonged." If you were the low sort of person who found his whimsicalities stupid—ditto, we thought the same of you; and probably deemed you a moral imbecile as well. We have changed a great deal since then. We are more broadminded, we tell ourselves.

But it was delightful moving only among people who loved *Mr. Blue,* while it lasted. He led one of us into Gethsemani; and two, or maybe it was three, into nunneries; and the rest of us, very congenial people, into matrimony. Probably influenced by the Blue plaint: "It's odd that nowadays there's no special appeal to sainthood for the heads of families." I said probably. . . .

* Myles Connolly, *Mr. Blue* (Macmillan).

That's why, I guess, when we found ourselves with that first extra twenty-dollar bill we put it between the covers of *Mr. Blue*. It was from tomatoes.

When my grandparents were very young the tomato was called the love apple. And, I suppose, the virus of Puritanism infecting everything good as it does, caused the people of that day to imagine that tomatoes were poisonous. Grandma used to raise them in her backyard but she'd never eat them. I always liked them.

But about that twenty-dollar bill. All that winter, before the time I'm talking about, city-farmer-wise, I read books on tomatoes, their kinds and culture. Early in February I had hotbeds planted, sixteen inches of horse-manure under eight inches of top-soil. I had put in tomato seed called "Victor." I felt pretty good about it.

That is, I felt pretty good about it, until I opened my big mouth after Mass one Sunday. My neighbors—they lived within a dozen miles of us, anyway—told me it was two weeks too early to plant tomato seed; twelve inches of manure was plenty, any more and I might burn the plants. Tomatoes weren't bringing any money the last couple of years. "Victor" was an inferior tomato, it grew ears and noses, and you couldn't sell them on the market, nohow. S'fact!

To cut a long story short: about the end of June that same year we had visitors. (On the farm you always have visitors.) It was a Friday, and we didn't have much in the house, and nothing to buy anything with anyway. Dot, good wife that she is, makes cream of tomato soup, sliced tomatoes around an omelet, and stewed tomatoes for a cooked vegetable. Being simple, as we really are, we apologized for the monotony of the meal, tomatoes on tomatoes. Our guests, amazed at such profusion, told us that tomatoes in the stores in town were selling at forty cents a pound when you could get them.

Our neighbors began telling their neighbors how much we were making on our two acres of tomatoes that summer. It wasn't ten thousand dollars! it was pretty close to one thousand.

Some of them did come around later with some show of respect and want to find out where I bought that "Victor" seed. And that's where we got the first twenty-dollar bill that we first put in *Mr. Blue.* That fall we paid the bank half of our indebtedness. I mean half of what we owed *them.*

And now a letter like this! Quoting fine print at the bottom of the note, to wit: "If any installment of this note is not paid at the time and place specified, the entire amount unpaid shall be due and payable at the election of the holder hereof." *Et cetera ad nauseam.*

"I thought that mortgage foreclosures only happened in plays written in the days of Victoria," says Dot.

"Probably because now in our enlightened era taking undue advantage of another for monetary profit is a respected business ethic. There is no matter for drama in it," said I Belloc-ishly. "But let's not spoil a good lunch talking of bankers and money. I'm hungry, and remember Mr. Blue's answer to the probability of his ending up in the poorhouse: 'That will be glorious, I have long known the magnificent possibilities of living in a poorhouse. I will become the troubadour of the poorhouse.' "

"Mr. Blue," states Dot shortly, stabbing at the butter, "did not have a wife and three children!"

And that was a point!

(A woman, it seems to me, is essentially practical. A

few simple words and one of them can puncture the
philosophical balloon of the male ego. Many years ago at
the University I was a vociferous exponent of Thoreau
and his *Walden,* and the simple life. One spring evening
a mere female sophomore from a sister college with whom
I happened to be walking exasperated me no end by
asking if Thoreau had ever married. The question was so
apt and unstudied it ruined the evening for me.) Blue
(nor Thoreau either) had no wife. It does make a difference, I guess.

So I seriously to her (my wife, not the sophomore)
said: "You're right. It makes a world of difference. When
you're married you've got to be practical. We'll have to
keep books religiously from now on. We must make a
budget and live up to it." I began to warm up to the
subject, a virtuous glow began to spread—but Dot inter-
jected this: "The trouble with a budget for us is we never
know how much we are going to make."

It was a point.

If you are living frugally, where can you cut down?
Unless we sell all our milk and cream like Seth Smith
(and the young Smiths need the doctor all the time, but
he doesn't have the money to have a doctor) and buy
canned milk from the grocer; sell all the wheat and buy
white bread at the chain-store in town. The budget is
out—that's not for such frugal, strong, and generous souls
as we, we said (I said).

"But tonight, we've got to sharpen our pencils and
start keeping books; add up all our debits and credits, if
any. Then we'll write another letter to the bank, and
make it business-like. Since they weren't interested in my
broken bones."

That being settled (a woman, my woman anyway,

always likes a conclusion reached no matter what it is), I went back to my plowing.

But about my broken bones: that's why we were presently "embarrassed financially," as the phrase goes. The truth is we had been sailing right smoothly, but didn't realize it. (You never think of the dentist until the tooth hurts; you never think of the veterinarian until the cow gets sick; you never really think of God until you want something.) One evening at chores I fell off the ladder leading to the hayloft, incapacitating myself to the extent of a broken arm and a dislocated shoulder. We thanked God that night after the doctor left that it was my shoulder and not my skull that hit the concrete floor. (I know I did anyway.)

Like any misfortune it was a valuable education. It gave me a chance to know my family, and catch up on reading. But we had to hire a man to help out for two months, and that is what put us in the hole. It couldn't have happened at a better time—we had just about cleaned up the fall work; and it was easy to borrow a hired man too. In spring or summer it would have been tragic.

Besides, spring, in any year, is a frugal time for the farmer: everything going out and nothing coming in.

What I've always loved the most about farming is the appetite I bring to the supper table. Dining by candlelight is what we do every night from necessity. I understand that in urban night-spots that is considered swank. "They sit half-goofed," says Dot (how she knows I would hesitate to imagine), "the candlelight on his bald head reflected in her eyes."

But at home, at our own handworked raw oak table, I'm a lord accepting the homage of three daughters and a tolerant wife. This may sound like rhetoric, but when you face the fact of losing something, the something assumes, I think, a true proportion. That must be hell. I mean, having lost heaven one first realizes what it is that is lost. And that's hell!

Supper over, dishes done, Rosary said, girls in bed, Dot looks at me and smiles. "Let's get on with our book-keeping."

The plain glass oil lamp, with its tin shade and reflector, made an island of mellow light on the table amid the shadows of the walls and ceiling. I took *Mr. Blue* from the bookshelf where he stood between a Modern Library edition of *Brothers Karamazov* on the right of him and a paper-covered Bernanos' *Journal d'un Curé de Campagne* on the left.

"Shoving all these papers and stuff in a book ruins it," I complained childishly as I emptied the papers and stuff on the table. Envelopes from the County Tax Office, envelopes from the Bank, envelopes from Soil Conservation Service, envelopes from Here, and envelopes from There. Dot was right when she said *Mr. Blue* was bulging.

Quoting Blue: "It's a black, bad business this money."

"Let's see now, we owe the bank a certain sum of money, some taxes, a doctor bill, something for fertilizer, a small item at the grocery, and a bit of a bill for fencing. That's our debits, our debts."

Credits: One (1) wife, sweet and beautiful and very good.

One (1) husband, faithful and doing his best.

Three (3) children, and one (1?) on the way. (God be praised.)

A small, compact house, some acres more or

F

less, a barn, henhouse, cows, chickens, an expectant sow, Fordson tractor, plows, harrows, some hay and grain, and other articles too numerous to mention,

as they say in those colored Farm Sale ads.

"Evidently we are not insolvent," says I.

"But definitely we are short on liquid assets," says she. But what to do?!

"Sell the cows?" To an accountant it was obviously the simple solution.

At the present price of steak we could more than pay our debts. . . .

But if the cows are sold, everything else except a few chickens might as well go. Our farm economy stood on the flanks of the cows. Our milk (cream and butter, not to mention the cream check every month) was our biggest income. The pigs grew sleek on their skim milk and corn diet. The corn gave heavy yields from cow manure. Sell the cows and go to work in town. That meant giving up farming: we might as well move to town, to be close to my place of work, shop, factory, store, or, maybe garbage-collecting, all honorable occupations, I trust.

But the accountant wouldn't know of the longings, the dreams, the sacrifices we went through to get a foothold on the land. He wouldn't know of the struggle and disappointments, the glory of every minor victory, the acquisition of each bit of experience. To the accountant we would say: "to hell with bankers and banks, if you'll pardon the expression."

Across the raw oak table littered with accounts payable, I expounded to Dot in a good pulpit style the conviction in our soul: "Farming for us is not a money-

making job; it's not a profession; it is more than a
vocation, or maybe you could call it a multiple-vocation.
A man's work is a vocation, if he is happy working for
the needs of others. Marriage is a vocation. The having
and rearing of children is a vocation. A vocation is a
calling from God enabling us to do our chosen work as
a path to Him, He being both the Way and the End. I
say, nowhere but on a farm can we be free, can we live
a full Christian family life with life-sustaining work for
me, for you, for the children; nowhere else is the voice of
God so close, the Way so free from distraction, the End
so easily attainable even on earth."

To work in town after a baker's dozen years of exciting
struggle (before and after marriage) because we lack
such a miserable sum of ready cash—the thought of it is
enough to nauseate both body and soul. The idea smells,
if you'll pardon the expression.

"Maybe we ought to write to the bank what you just
said about farming," Dot said hopefully, "it sounded
awfully moving."

"Mammon wouldn't understand it. The first sentence
would cause apoplexy."

"In a month the tomatoes and peppers will be ready
for market. But the bank wants the three hundred dollars now, pronto, immedjut! The pigs are only about
eighty pounds or so—that means the cows, two of them
anyway."

> "For the want of a horseshoe
> A kingdom was lost . . . nuts!"

"We don't need a horseshoe—we want a miracle. Let's
start praying."

Our night prayers took a little longer than usual that

evening, and my knees were awfully stiff as I climbed into bed (that Fordson is a man-killer).

The next morning we decided I had better go to town and see if I could talk the bank into a more patient frame of mind, or at least find out the worst.

"You might as well cash the check Susie got for her birthday while you're there. And buy her a coloring book and some crayons." Dorothy walked over to *Mr. Blue* and took the check. It was a cashier's check for five dollars from her god-father—a sort of uncle. He had written on the birthday card: "Dear Susan, tell your Mommy and Daddy they can spend this on anything they want. Best wishes. 'Uncle' Joe." A good Joe, with literary aspirations, and an ardent admirer of Mr. Blue, and that is why we asked him to be Sue's god-father.

When I got to the bank Mr. Dick, the loan officer, was busy. So I went over to the teller to cash Susie's check.

"How do you want this?" he asked.

"Ones will be all right," I answered.

"What?" he asked with a startled look.

"Why?" I inquired.

"Five hundred ones will make quite a bundle."

"Five hundred? That's a five-dollar check."

"This check," the cashier informed me in a coldly professional tone, "is a five-hundred-dollar check."

With a trembling hand I reached for that check. Sure enough, there was the 500 in red followed by two black 00. But the way the mechanical check-writer chewed into the paper only the red 500 showed up plainly.

"Well, what do you know?" I gasped, but felt like shouting it. "In that case I want to pay these installments on the loan," I said, pulling out my loan book, "and give me the change in tens!"

I wanted to phone Dot and shout the good news, only we don't have a phone.

I bought Susie's birthday present, a velocipede, a huge red one. When Dorothy saw me dragging it from the jaloppy she thought that worry over the loan had unbalanced my mind, and she rushed from the house with a worried look. After some kissing and dancing her around the barnyard I managed to convey the news of the miracle so she could grasp it.

"But the tricycle," she pointed out. "Sue won't be able to ride that for years."

"Oh well," I said, "it will be something around the house to remind us of the miracle."

OUR TWO FAMILIES

∾

MOLLY WALSH

SPEAKING OF THE 1930s inevitably conjures up pictures of the all-pervading fact of unemployment, of the bands of unemployed Welsh miners who moved around the West End of London singing their native songs, of queues at unemployment exchanges, above all of the marches and demonstrations and stirring up of the masses by the Communists and their friends.

It was in this atmosphere that the English *Catholic Worker* was born. It seemed to grow spontaneously from groups disturbed by the predicament of the workers in four or five areas of the industrial North and in London. Bob, my husband, became Editor when it was six months old.

In London, *Catholic Worker* sellers were out in force at all the Communist rallies and demonstrations. In Hyde Park and Trafalgar Square we sold the paper, argued and counter-demonstrated. It is odd, looking back, how suddenly, we—Bob and I—were seized with the revolutionary fever. One moment we were ordinary London suburban dwellers rather pleased with ourselves that after five years' engagement we had scraped together enough money to furnish a small flat and get married, the next we were part of the revolutionary mob. True, it was the Catholic version of the revolution that we were eager to "get across," and Dorothy Day, the wonderful New York convert from Communism, who was our inspiration and spiritual leader, but there is no denying that forces outside our ordinary selves had us in their grip.

It appeared the height of imprudence that in this mood we should decide to change the whole pattern of our lives and answer an appeal made by a Wigan priest for a married couple to live in and help to manage a "House of Hospitality" which he had started.

It was an imprudence which we have never regretted. Because, though God might very easily have said, "You got yourselves into this mess, it will do you good to suffer for it," in fact He never did. Every muddle which arose from trying to fit a young family into the framework of a House of Hospitality was untangled for us quite unexpectedly, in ways which we ourselves could never have foreseen nor worked out. Neither the work which the group in the House was doing, nor the family, suffered in the process.

What is a typical House of Hospitality? The term was coined by Dorothy Day and Peter Maurin. Dorothy, as I have said, had been a Communist, and on her conversion she and Peter joined forces to formulate a Catholic answer to the Communist propaganda. She and Peter and the first people who came to help them with the publication of the American *Catholic Worker*—the parent of all the *Catholic Workers* and similar publications throughout the world—lived a communal life in which all contributed to the daily living necessities according to their means, and all shared the common food and lodging. To these were added various unfortunate people whom the group took under their wing and to whom they gave food and shelter. Soon similar places were springing up all over the U.S.A. and Canada. Fr. Rimmer's was the first in England.

Wigan was one of the very badly hit industrial towns in Northern England. More than one third of the men were unemployed in 1933, and the numbers grew weekly. Fr. Rimmer, fresh from the seminary, was horrified with the problems which faced him in his first curacy. He was given charge of the Men's Guild. But what could he say or do for these men, faced with an unrelieved prospect of unwanted, poverty-stricken leisure?

He realized that the crying need was to fill those weary days. First he formed a study circle to study the Encyclicals and Catholic social doctrine. When he came across a copy of the *Catholic Worker,* he sent for bundles, and the men sold them around the town.

Then he read of the American Houses of Hospitality, and he decided that he would open one to help the families in the town and to offer hospitality to the many men who then walked the roads of England hoping to find work somewhere.

He set the men to recondition a dilapidated shop and house. All was ready for the opening when the first snag was met. The Archbishop of Liverpool insisted that a married couple must be responsible for the house. Fr. Rimmer advertised in the Catholic press, and it was in answer to this appeal that we came.

The approach to Wigan by railway is dreary in the extreme. Past great slag heaps, beyond which one catches glimpses of blackened water left through mining subsidence and known as the flashes, past rows upon rows of monotonous, smoke-grimed cottages, considered in the nineteenth century "excellent workmen's dwellings," the train slides into view of the gasworks and crawls to a stop in the station. That gasworks was to be quite a cross to me in my first year in Wigan.

When we arrived, typically, it was raining. Trade was so depressed that most of the shops around were unused. The first sight of the House, in spite of all the hard work that had been done on it, was not inspiring to tired eyes. The first impression was of a very crowded junk shop— this was due to the miscellaneous articles that people had sent in to be given to the unemployed as soon as we should start work. Beyond this was a room which had no window of any sort—the whole premises were the worst planned I have ever come across. Beyond this again was the kitchen-living room—this was clean and brightly painted but looked very cold and bare that first night. It became cosy and homely when the fire was lit and a few homemade rugs put on the floor.

Upstairs, however, in the room which was to be our bed-sitting room—not that there was ever any time to sit!—a real Lancashire tea had been prepared, and eight or nine of the men who had done the spade work on the House were there to greet us. Over this welcome meal began a lasting friendship with the unemployed—mostly miners—who were to be our co-workers.

Into this framework we started to fit our family life, for within a few weeks of arriving in Wigan I found I was pregnant.

The first few months were not easy. For one thing the change in the atmosphere was little short of dramatic. In London we had lived in a fever of excitement. The constant travelling about, the arguments, the mounting

sales of the paper, the heady songs of the demonstrators
in Hyde Park to which we replied with silent prayer,
gave us a quite spurious feeling of apostolic fervor which
was none the less very exhilarating. But though we were
young enough thoroughly to enjoy this excitement, we
knew in our hearts that it had nothing permanent to offer
to relieve the misery of the masses. The feeling that
truth had so little chance of being heard among the
clamorous voices in the market place made us desire
somehow to become part of this suffering world, to share
the sufferings, to create somewhere a place where
Christianity was being tried, so that if by chance we were
challenged, "Where does He live, this Jesus of Nazareth?", we could say, "Come and see!" For various reasons, the London group had not favored the immediate
founding of a House of Hospitality in London, so that
Fr. Rimmer's advertisement seemed an answer to our
bewilderment. But in Wigan, unemployment did not
mean demonstrations and marches and revolutionary
songs. It meant for the men long empty days. Even the
cigarette which their fretted nerves demanded was only
a "dole day" treat. For the women it meant empty
houses—all useless furniture had to be sold before the
"Means Test Man" would recommend them for relief—
it meant a weary dragging out of resources from one
meagre pay day to the next. And the continual, nagging,
heartbreaking problem, how to keep backs covered and
feet shod. And these were proud women, who had prided
themselves on their comfortable homes and tidy children, to whom debt was a disgrace, and the continual
battle to fight the grimy atmosphere of industrial Wigan
and prevent it encroaching in the house taken as a matter
of course. Even the flagstones outside the front doors are
scrubbed right down to the curb in Wigan.

We had wanted to become part of the masses. God took us at our word. The excitement went and the dreariness took hold of us. Instead of our feeling that we were doing something rather grand, the utter impossibility of touching even the fringes of the wants of those hard-pressed Wigan women became daily more apparent to us. In the first few weeks before any way of life had been evolved, all day long a procession of shawled women came to tell us of their needs. They showed us the children's broken shoes, legs blue with cold because they had no stockings, pitiful thin, patched frocks and coats. And the recurring cry, I am expecting in a week, or a month or two months and I just don't know how I am going to get any nappies, or little gowns—all the things which it has always been women's loving pride to store away awaiting the time of their deliverance.

From the beginning too, a group of people began to form who must be fed daily. There were first of all the men who had begun to help Bob in the office. When dinner time came round, no one made a move to go. They all said it was not worth going home in the rain and coming back, they'd "wait till tea time." I gave them tea and bread and butter. In a week or so, when I began to visit them in their homes, I soon discovered that in the homes of unemployed men there was no dinner time that you could notice. As soon as I discovered this, I began to make every day a large pot of stew. Meat and vegetables were very cheap, and a good hot meal that served all who came could be made at small expense. At first it was hard to persuade them to accept anything, and it was only by assuring them that I had made too much that their pride was overcome and they consented to stay.

Very soon the midday meal began to be a very important function in the House of Hospitality. The group was swelled first of all by a few real outcasts of the town—there was, for instance, "Don" (which was not his name, but it will serve).

He was an undersized, unkempt, ageless little gnome of a man. His wife was dead, he was addicted to drink, and he used to spend his time hanging around the market in Wigan. He first of all used to drop in just after dinner and would accept a cup of tea. When eventually I persuaded him to stop for meals with us, he insisted on giving me every week a sum of money out of his dole. He delighted in talking in Lancashire dialect so broad that we could not understand what he said. From Friday to Monday he never appeared at the House, and we soon discovered that he spent what was left of his dole on drink. We made efforts to reform him, but it had too strong a hold of him, and in spite of many good resolutions he finally succumbed completely, got into arrears with his rent and disappeared from the town.

Bill was a professional tramp but had been in hospital and was too weak, for the time, to continue his journeyings. He was very clean and a wonderful help in the kitchen, but had a terrible temper. Then there was John, an orphan, who has been with us ever since.

Other men would come to do various jobs—trying to mend the many leaks in the roof, knock up a rough cupboard here or a screen there—and some would stay for dinner. There would be visiting priests and university students and professors, and tramps—sometimes of the incorrigible wandering type, who were tramps from the very restlessness of the spirit; sometimes, infinitely more pathetic, men who had either lost their homes through some entanglement of the laws of drawing relief, or were doggedly tramping the roads in the hopes of finding work somewhere—a very forlorn hope in those days.

The discussions which took place over dinner became a feature which persisted all through the life of the House of Hospitality. Everything under the sun was discussed. The Spanish civil war, Communism and Fascism, the Old Testament and the New and every point of doctrine. And the ever varying group of people that sat down every day were somehow always a family group. Dinner time never lasted less than two hours.

So life began to take form. Mornings were taken up for me with shopping and preparing the midday meal. A few women came in during the morning, though I was gradually trying to direct the distribution of clothes to the afternoon. After dinner a continual stream of women came in, and I struggled to fit their needs as regards clothing or make notes of them for future consideration when more clothing was available.

Evenings were taken up with formal discussion groups led by professors from Upholland College. We attempted quite an ambitious adult education course in philosophy, theology, social science, etc., and all the lectures were crowded.

This, then, was the typical life in a House of Hospitality. It grew quite spontaneously from the needs we found in Wigan, but later I was repeatedly told by visitors from the United States that it was typical of a score of other such Houses in the States and Canada.

Our coming to Wigan was an act of faith in God's Providence. And as I have said, although it was done in a mood of perhaps imprudent fervor, God accepted our dependence upon Him. At the time we left London the paper had barely enough money coming in to pay printing and distribution costs. We knew that shelter was assured us, as the House of Hospitality Committee were paying the rent and light bills. Before we left London we had been living for the last few months on my salary as secretary to a doctor.

We had vaguely thought Bob might be able to make enough to feed us by free-lance journalism. I cannot remember where the housekeeping money came from the first few weeks we were in Wigan. We had sold some of our furniture before we came up, and possibly there were a few pounds left. At the next Editorial Board meeting, however, we were voted £1 a week for "expenses," and this fed us and the growing House of Hospitality family for the next few months. Clothes had not become a problem, as we had sufficient to last a while. We soon found that Bob had very little time for "free-lance" journalism, even if he could have found a market for it. Shortly after our arrival in Wigan, the Manager of the paper, Eileen Wall, had to give up through ill health, and Bob undertook the full work of the paper, which was rapidly expanding and which, with the work of the Enquiry Bureau—part of the work of the House of Hospitality—more than occupied all his time.

I have no miracles to record, no multiplications of food, only always enough for all who came. True, once when we thought there was an overdraft on the *Catholic Worker* account there turned out to be a balance—but that was bad bookkeeping! But the problems were numerous. It was really a shocking house; it leaked all over the place, the sanitation was bad. There were not nearly enough rooms for all the activities. And into this house had to be fitted our growing family.

Often I worried, being that way inclined. Who would

do the cooking, smooth over the little clashes of temperament in such a diverse household, and attend to the distribution of clothes when my time came? Where could the baby be born? That house was no place for a confinement.

It all worked out. I had made friends with a lonely old lady. After a lifetime of hardship she was left without family in Wigan, and I used to go and have a cup of tea with her and listen to her reminiscences. She was thrilled with the news of my baby. A new light came into her eye, a new interest into her life. She offered me hospitality in her little house. She would see to everything. First we must see the Relieving Officer and tell him she was doing it for love and not for payment—but once that was settled, all was plain sailing. We furnished her little front parlour with necessities, and all I had to do was to continue with my work until my time came—she lived only a few minutes' walk away.

In due course, again unexpectedly, Mary Power, a London seller of the paper, wrote and asked if she could join us—at that time she thought only temporarily—and with my sister's help she managed the House when my confinement took place.

So, without any upset at all, on 25th August 1937, John Francis was born—just as the gasworks hooter was blowing eight o'clock.

I count it as not the least of God's blessings to me that my babies were born in Actons Walk—I was subsequently to have two more babies in that small parlour. A fourth, born in the war years, was born in hospital, and I know what I would have missed if God had not brought Mrs. Hughes and me together. It was in her house that I experienced the natural sense of community which exists among the very poor, and the way in which they rally around each other in the crises of birth, illness and death.

All the neighbors did something for us during the time I was in bed. A knock would come on the door, and a cup of soup or gruel—sometimes a complete meal—would be brought in. They helped with the washing, they made things for the baby. John Francis's journey to be baptized was quite a triumphal tour.

Meanwhile the work went on uninterruptedly at the House. The men took over the cooking, Mary and my sister Janet dealt with the distribution of clothes. But I still had not learnt to stop worrying; I wondered how I would manage when I returned to work at the House and had the baby to look after as well. Of course, my worrying was quite unnecessary. Mary decided to stay permanently, and with her help at the House and Mrs. Hughes' help with the baby's washing we soon evolved a routine in which everything went on as before.

The problem of housing then became acute. We had quite outgrown the House, and in the poorer quarters of the town where we wanted to be, there just did not seem to be any large houses. We first of all rented an extra house, but it was just far enough away to disturb the family atmosphere and turned out to be very badly bug-infested. We spent a very uncomfortable few months. But suddenly, when we had nearly given up hope, by some inexplicable whim on my part, instead of taking John Francis to the park for his afternoon walk, I decided to visit a church which was somewhat off our usual track, and there I discovered a large house and shop to let. It had been specially built to meet the needs of a family business, and it had all our immediate requirements, including—joy of joys!—a bathroom and a hot-water system in good working order.

Beryl Manthorne from Ipswich had now joined our permanent staff. Finances were again becoming an acute problem. But once more, without any request from us, the Board of the paper offered us a rise, and again it was just sufficient to meet the household needs, living in a very frugal way, though we were all dependent on charity for the replacement of clothes. However, the necessary minimum always turned up.

The autumn of 1938 brought the Munich crisis. Like everyone else we queued for gas masks. Bob was in America, but the rest of us organized prayers for peace. We also duplicated and distributed a large number of copies of *Prayers for Peace,* which we got from a small book of such prayers which Sheed & Ward published that year. The work at the House was getting heavier all the time, and I was once more expecting a baby, but I look back on it as a time of great happiness. Not that we did not have troubles, of course we did. But Our Lord gave us abundant proof of the validity of his promise, "Where two or three are gathered together in my name, there am I in the midst of you." That, I think, was the abiding feeling of all of us who lived and worked in the House of Hospitality. It was rather an embarrassment when visitors came and expected to find a group of people advanced in holiness and found instead only a miscellaneous group of very ordinary people who had decided to take Our Lord seriously when He said that they who served the poor served Him. But in spite of all our weaknesses—and they were very many—because the poor were entertained with honor in the House, Our Lord somehow was there too. And again, the visitors

G

from the United States who were becoming quite frequent told us that this was found in all the various
Houses of Hospitality.

Christmas was a time of exceptional busyness for us.
People made an extra effort to send clothes, toys and
money to buy food for the families we could help, and
that Christmas was especially fruitful.

The birth of my second baby, Michael Joseph, brought
another trial for our faith. Up to that time our family life
had fitted in with the life of the household. John Francis
had been a placid child and had contentedly played
around wherever I happened to be working, but Michael
was a delicate baby and I had to spend much time and
anxious attention on him, and now that John Francis
was getting older he was beginning to need some separate family life. We decided that he must have his
evening meal in our room with Bob and me. This and
the baby left me very little time for the other half of
my family—the House of Hospitality—and threw considerable strain on Mary Power, who was never very strong.

It seemed as if a real weakness in our life had been
discovered, and something must crack. But I think it
would have broken our hearts to give up at this juncture.
The people were as badly in need as ever, and an ever
growing list of expectant mothers and invalids had come
to look to us for a little extra nourishment, etc. All the
people thus helped were known and loved. It would have
been like abandoning one's own family in a crisis.

As usual, out of the blue came the answer, quite complete. Mary O'Malley, who was a children's nurse, wrote
to say that she had been so happy in the House during
a few days' stay she had made at Christmas that she
would like to come back as a helper, but she did not

want to give up her work with babies—could she mind mine? I might add that children's nurses were very hard to get at that time and that many people able to pay highly could not obtain one.

Once more we got into our stride. The people living in the house—sometimes we had to borrow bedrooms from the neighbors—were generally about twelve, and the number to the midday meal about twenty.

I think here is the place to mention that, although as John Francis became older and more sensitive it had become necessary to modify our life to some extent (that is, we had to set aside certain times to being alone with the children), our family life never in any way suffered from the community life, nor were Bob and I ever less than completely members of the little community because of our family life. In fact we had a kind of joint membership which was completely satisfactory.

If it had been necessary, I am sure that as the children grew older further modifications could have been made which would have made it possible to pursue the dual role. I am quite certain God gave special graces both to Bob and me and to the other members of the community to make this situation possible, and if circumstances had made it necessary He would have continued to give us those Graces.

However, in September that year the war came, and very soon, after the crazy pattern of this civilization, prosperity came to the town and has not forsaken it again —yet.

The war saw the gradual break-up of our little community. The men were very soon called up or absorbed into the manufacture of munitions. Mary O'Malley returned to Ireland. In June Bob was called up, and the probability—soon to become fact—of air raids on London made it necessary for me to bring my parents up north. Mary Power and I were the only ones left of the community. The possibility of air raids in Wigan also, and the desire to try to continue to provide eggs and what else we could for some old people and invalids, decided us to take a cottage in the country with a couple of acres of ground.

Even at this time, a year after the beginning of the war, there was still much poverty in Wigan. At the beginning of the war family allowances for soldiers were very small, and this, following years of unemployment, often left the need for clothing in large families quite urgent. So Mary Power decided to stop on in Wigan—the cottage was only three miles outside, so I could get in to help and she could come out at week-ends. Actually, it was a great wrench for me to leave the house which I felt Our Lady had found for us, and I have often wondered if this was a wrong move. It meant that Mary and I split our forces, and after a year during which there were many sleepless nights, owing to air raid alerts, she had to give up. She continued to edit the *Catholic Worker*, but for a while did so from her home in Norwich.

From then till the end of the war, Garden Cottage was the House of Hospitality. It was only a four-roomed cottage, but it was amazing the number of people it sheltered at times. When Wigan was nightly disturbed with air raid alerts several of our friends came out for a good night's rest. Various evacuated families made their home with us from time to time. A little girl came to live with us whilst her mother worked in munitions. Different people came for various lengths of time, suffering from various forms of nerve strain due to the war.

Thanks, most certainly, to God's providence, we were very successful in our gardening operations, and with the produce from the garden and the goodness of a friend in America all the inhabitants of the cottage fared very well for wartime England, and we were able to continue to help a few invalids and old people as well.

The whole of the wartime period was a very busy one. Sorrow visited us: one of my babies died, and Mary Power lost her mother. Joy, also, in Mary's marriage to an American soldier and worker for the Catholic Worker movement and the birth of her first baby (she has four now). And I was consoled when my third son was born.

And through it all the *Catholic Worker* was produced somehow. When Mary was sick I was well; when I was laid up with phlebitis after the birth of my third baby, she took over at the cottage for a time; and when she had to leave, the near-miraculous, for that time, happened. A qualified cook who had been suffering from a severe nervous breakdown offered her services free. It happened that at that time there were only my parents and my family "in residence." She was a wonderful help, and I had a complete rest with an easy mind till I was well again.

Glancing back through this essay, it seems to be a catalogue of our doings rather than what I wanted it to be—a record of God's care of us, and as such the story may sound dull. Not being an artist, I cannot depict that Providence. Worry and oversolicitousness are very hard things to kill. Confidence in our Lord's promise that if we would choose first the Kingdom of Heaven these things would be added, is a flower very hard to grow in the hard soil of our faithlessness. But in spite of the stoniness of the ground, God has patiently tended and watered this flower in us.

We can claim no single reason why He should have done this, only His own goodness. The first step of coming to Wigan was not really the fruit of virtue on our part, but only of the heady atmosphere in which we found ourselves. But God took even this unworthy thing and changed it into something which He could use.

This is the age of the Lay Apostolate. The lesson of the various Catholic Worker movements, of which our little effort was only a small spark thrown out by a much greater flame, is that the Apostolate can be made a way of life even if one has the responsibility of a family.

Since the end of the war our Catholic Worker has not been able to find a suitable house to continue its activities in any sort of comunity. The kind of work we did in the House of Hospitality has not so far become necessary in post-war England. But in God's good time, I feel sure that He will allow us to use this gift which He gratuitously gave us for the furtherance of His Kingdom.

ABANDONMENT

J. E. P. BUTLER

I WAS BORN with lead in my feet. My father used to offer me pennies to try to make me run. Just when I learned to hurry I do not know, but when I did I couldn't stop. I couldn't wait for anything, even God. Twenty-three years ago I had completed an intensive course in ascetic theology, made an act of absolute abandonment to the divine will, and got ready to go to Heaven, in a hurry. I had a lot to learn. I had learned how to die. I still had to learn how to live. But the surrender, it seems, was real, and all else, as a consequence, greatly simplified.

It has occurred to me that out of this topsy-turvy adventure in Christian perfection wiser persons might draw comfort in a topsy-turvy world. The ascetics put abandonment at the end of the book. That, of course, is where it belongs. But how long is the book? We never know, and for many in our time it is very short indeed. Also in our time there are many for whom life is more difficult than death. For persons possessed of any degree of sensibility the world today is pretty hard to take. How best can we take it?

The case for abandonment is this. It cuts the Gordian Knot. It solves the whole complex problem of human existence at one stroke. He who lives in absolute abandonment to the will of God shares in the power and wisdom of God. He can know or do anything God wills him to do. He has no desire to know or do anything else. Superficially nothing is changed. Superficially we think as before, act as before. Superficially things are, if anything, more difficult than before. *Substantially God has taken over.* And the substance begins to appear in a pattern. We find that we are doing better than we know. We perceive that we are being deflected from wrong courses, guided into right. We realize that we are meeting challenge after challenge beyond the competence of autonomy.

Today the heart of the world is breaking. How shall we find peace? I believe that our consolation, our peace of mind, perhaps even our very sanity, depends on complete surrender to the will of God. Each of us must be able to say in all simplicity: "I would suffer what it is Thy will that I should suffer. I would do what it is Thy will that I should do. Possess my will, that I may have no will but Thine."

Perhaps I should say here that I speak as a layman to laymen. When I first embraced the doctrine of abandonment I had not intended to marry, but almost immediately the pattern that was to include marriage began to appear.

About this time, twenty-three years ago, it was given me to comfort a man who was dying of abdominal cancer. As a consequence I was asked to visit a girl some distance away who was in an advanced stage of tuberculosis. In the case of the man I had not attempted in-

struction. In fact I did nothing that I know. I know only
that he wanted me there. He suffered horribly and died
gloriously—what price euthanasia? With the girl I did
begin instruction, and unexpectedly she also began to
improve in health. Four years later she was out of bed,
and two years after that we were married. (Repeated
breakdowns had destroyed my hope of a religious or
priestly vocation.) After five years of marriage her first
pregnancy brought a return of her disease and she died,
three days after the birth of our only child. The birth was
Caesarian, done under a local anaesthetic. She had a fine
humor, and in the operating room put on a splendid
performance which she ended by threatening twins next
time. I did not need to discover, as I did later, that before
she went to the hospital she had written out on a
scratchpad an acceptance of death.

Since then I have been housekeeper and nurse, teacher
and breadwinner to our child. I mixed her formula and
changed her diapers. I put her through the first four
grades at home in two years. She has just completed
the eighth grade at the head of her class. The second
four grades have been done at the nearest convent. I did
not choose to teach her. I had to. We were too far from
a decent school. I didn't push her. She set her own pace.
She was given a chance. That is all. She is entering
Grade IX at twelve instead of fourteen, and I'm not at
all sure it shouldn't be the rule instead of the exception.

Let these personal paragraphs illustrate the life and
the pattern. We suffer what is given us to suffer. We do
what is given to us to do. For that which is given us to
suffer and to do is the manifest will of God. It is so simple
I believe that many good people must live the doctrine
without knowing it, but somehow, consciously or uncon-

sciously, sooner or later, must come the transference, the whole and final surrender to providence. For the simple it may be simple. For many of us it is anything but simple. The act of abandonment is an act of simplicity, and before we can achieve it we must achieve simplicity. "Unless you become like unto little children, you shall not enter the kingdom of God."

Whoever would pursue this matter further should procure some work on ascetic theology. My own favorite book was the *Holy Wisdom* of Father Augustine Baker, a Benedictine who served the English mission in the Post-Reformation period.

I proceed with extreme diffidence to indicate an approach to abandonment. The memory of my own approach is dim, and I have made no recent study. We propose to submit ourselves to God. Who is God, and what are we? God is our Father and we are His children, and if we could say the *Our Father* perfectly we should ourselves be perfect, and there would be nothing more to say. Let him who despises the anthropomorphic concept remember that. We know that God is not man. We know that He *is*, and is nothing that we know. But we know that Christ is God, and we know that Christ is man, and on the word of Christ, we are the sons of God. God is our Father, Who is Power and Wisdom, Justice and Mercy and Love. If anyone says that God is too great to attend to us, heed him not, for greatness has escaped him. Only the great regard the little. The poet despises not the comma, nor God the least of His work. God is our Father and we are His children, and we owe Him what children owe a father, but in infinite degree.

What is it we owe to our Father Who is God? I might call it love, but I shall call it obedience. Until lovers learn obedience they do not know the meaning of love. It is obedience that makes love, love of the master and love of the fellow-servant. That is why the end of a good marriage is better than its beginning. Indeed an honest marriage *is* an act of abandonment, because it is the final acceptance without reservation of the privations and duties, together with the consolations, of a state of life. I say that it is *an* act of abandonment. I do not say it is *the* act. But marriage is often so complete a vocation that for many it may indeed constitute that perfection of obedience we call abandonment.

How do we arrive at the state of abandonment? Abandonment is whole obedience, and we achieve it by the practice of partial obedience. We make particular acts regarding particular trials and obligations, actual or potential, and we make general acts excepting things we think we cannot take. As we continue our strength increases, the exceptions are fewer, and in God's good time we achieve the complete surrender. (Father Baker's book is particularly useful in that it gives many pages of model acts.) We presuppose the state of grace—and here a word to the scrupulous. You do not know whether you are in the state of grace. You never *will* know. Gather together the pieces of your shattered will. Decide to proceed on the assumption that you *are* in the state of grace. A gamble? Why not? What have you got to lose? You have all of God to gain. You can do this, and I do not see how you can do better.

I do not wish to make this more difficult than it is, but because it seems easy in retrospect there is danger that I may make it easier than it is. Remember that we are preparing a treaty of peace with God. The terms of that treaty will be complete surrender in exchange for complete security. We cannot do it all ourselves. We cannot do our own part but by God's grace, and we cannot do God's part at all. We must not be discouraged by the implications of this, but also we must not disregard them, or we shall be in danger of serious self-deception with consequent delay or failure. All the strength of our nature is required for this act, and it is the least that is required. We must storm Heaven itself for the grace of surrender, and God's acceptance of that surrender. I remember that among other things I walked to daily Mass and Communion four miles each way, month after month, year after year, in every kind of weather. That was probably the deciding factor. You are safe with Mass and Communion.

Do not on any consideration indulge in flagellation, extreme fasts or any thing of that sort. Such things are justified only by special sanction, which we dare not take for granted, and otherwise can do only harm. There are conditions under which even daily Mass may not be justified. For instance, a mother would not be justified in neglecting her children, nor a father the labor of providing for his family. Our whole business is the *perfection of duty*, and this cannot possibly be accomplished by the neglect of duty. If you are wholly occupied with essential duty, the battle, if not already won, is certainly in your favor. "God, take this duty, make it Thine. It is all I have to give. I know that if by Thy grace it is perfect, it is all I need to give. Possess me wholly that I may fail in nothing that is required of me. Thy will be done."

What is the proof that we have achieved abandonment? There is no immediate proof, and this side of Heaven there is no final proof, but the proof that we have is sufficient. It is the emergence of the pattern, a chain of causality leading link by link from good to good through evil upon evil. We see that we are taking it, that we are coming through, and the knowledge of what we are taking and how we are coming through will fill us to overflowing with humility, gratitude and love. There is nothing romantic about this. On the contrary, we approach the very Source of reality. Understand what it is that you have done. You have delivered yourself into God's hands that He may have His Will with you. You will learn that His Will is very wonderful and very terrible.

You will suffer as you had not thought it possible to suffer, and you will not get used to suffering, because then it would not be suffering. There may be times when you will say: "This is not abandonment. This is despair. This is Hell." And until it passes you cannot know that it is not Hell. You have sometimes said: "If I were in Purgatory, I should be safe." But you did not know what you said, for now you are safe, and this is purgation. Though you do not know it now, it is because you are safe that you can suffer these things. You are under the hands of the Surgeon, excising, cauterizing, wounding that He may heal. You are being smelted and forged, ground and polished, that you may be fit for the house of God. Excluding Hell, whether by way of abandonment, or by any other way, there is no escape from this, and the way of abandonment is easiest because it is quick and sure. There is no waste of time or effort, because *God* knows what He does.

All this is the merest summary, and I shall write no book. There are many books. There will be others. And whatever books you use must be adapted to your particular need. Even in so brief a script as this there may be things that do not apply. For example, I believe that there are very gentle people with whom God deals very gently, more gently than this article would indicate. Let not such be afraid. Ultimately your salvation is between you and God. Trust *Him*. Cultivate by every means at your disposal the habit of religious obedience till you arrive at that absolute obedience where God assumes the burden. Here is the only real security. "In His Will is our Peace." *Orate pro me*.

FLIGHT INTO EGYPT

❧

D. H.

I AM OFTEN ASKED: How did you come here? and I find the question difficult to answer. I could say: by ship, or, with an I.R.O. pass, or, on the D.P. quota; but such an answer, though factually the truth, would be almost meaningless in my own mind: what would it convey of my unforgettable experience—the exodus through bombardments and artillery fire, with a baby in my arms and three small children clinging to me; the long, homeless years—but, most inexpressible, the wonder of being here in America with four healthy, happy children? The real answer is: God led us here, step by step, and this journey is what I am going to try to describe.

Have you ever been in Budapest? Do you remember the Danube, the mighty river which separates the business town, Pest, from romantic Buda? We lived in Buda, in a quiet villa which gave me a splendid view of the surrounding hills, as well as the Danube and the Royal Castle. When I shut my eyes I can still see the big cupola of the Castle, the crown of Saint Stephen sparkling on it, and, looking to the right, the pink blossoms of the almond trees on Saint Gellert's Hill. I can hear the sounds of an April morning—birds, bees and children's laughter, seldom interrupted by the roar of a motor—and feel the warmth of the sun shining into our happy home.

It was a happy home, and we lived in it in what we thought perfect security. The center of our life was the nursery where, after the little girl came a little boy, and then another little boy. They were all healthy and lively, and of course we thanked God for them. But when I think back, I feel that we did not thank Him as deeply as we should have, nor did we ask Him to protect our home as intently as we should have, because we took everything for granted. We did not see things as we see them today—and we did not feel God's presence as we have so often since. We went to Mass each Sunday, said our prayers regularly, gave our share to the poor, and, with this, thought we were fulfilling our religious duties and were good Catholics. We did not feel the urge of speaking to God, and trying to hear His voice. We did not reach for Him out of the warm, comfortable shelter of our happy home. But He thought of us, and when everything around us went up in flames, when our life was as secure as that of a trapped hare, He spoke to us and let us hold onto Him for safety. Therefore, when I think over the past—and I like to do it because of all the lovely memories I have—I do not feel any regret. Our losses were purely material, and in exchange for them we got the chance to come closer to God, to feel the gratitude due Him for our daily bread; we learned to be unworried and light of heart like the lilies of the field and the birds of heaven.

The first change in our life came one morning in early March. It was a beautiful morning and I walked to town. Little islands of ice were floating on the Danube, but spring was already in the air and an old man was selling violets on St. Elizabeth bridge. I bought a bunch, fastened it on my 'fur coat, and thought of the things I wanted to buy. But I was never to buy them, because just as I turned into the smart shopping street, the sirens blew. All traffic stopped. I could not go home, but had to go to the next shelter and wait. Wait for the planes to come, the bombs to fall; wait for death here, to me and my unborn child, or there to my children and husband. Or wait perhaps, simply for the "all clear." After an hour the "all clear" sounded, but in that hour of terror and hope I had learned to see life with different eyes. I was no longer thinking of dresses and hats—only of the children, my husband, all my loved ones—and saying in my heart: "God, oh God, wilt Thou hear me, though it needed this blow to turn my heart to Thee?" He heard me and gave me assurance and tranquility. When I went home, I knew what we had to do. We packed during the night and took the early morning train to my mother's place. It was there that we learned, next morning, that hardly an hour after our departure the Germans entered and occupied the city. Ours was the last train to leave. Bombardments were now imminent. I was full of gratitude that I had been warned.

Seven hundred years ago, the Mongols of the Great Khan invaded Hungary. After a disastrous defeat the King fled the battlefield. One of his followers got lost, and after much wandering found sanctuary in a well-hidden spot of earth surrounded by woods and marshland. This man was my ancestor, and this same spot of land now sheltered our children. Generations had changed it into a little paradise. Woods and marshes were now only a picturesque touch in the landscape, but

H

it was still a well-hidden place. No railway and no main road passed the village, and the Germans overlooked it, so we had no enemy occupation, no air raids, but peace and beauty around us.

We did not know then that this was the last summer for the Old Place, nor that in hardly a year's time, we should be wandering in a foreign country and sleeping out of doors. But He Who knew it, let the Old Place give its best for the last time, and lavish on the children in plenty all that they were going to miss in the future.

The roses—soon to be crushed down by tanks—bloomed more abundantly than ever; the orchard—where not one tree was to be spared—bore more fruit than in any other year; the melons—the last that grew for us on this beloved soil—were sweet as sugar. Even the old Delaware vinestock—kept as a dear souvenir of the times when it had covered the old-fashioned arbor—produced a few grapes, as if to satisfy the children's curiosity concerning itself and draw their attention to its interesting name. I told them about the great Delaware river, and of the country in which it flowed. They enjoyed my story, as they enjoyed everything in the Old Place. The complete freedom of this real home, the affection of the big family, gave them a foundation of happy confidence which they were to keep during the homeless years to come, when they were continually being hush-hushed because of impatient landlords and unfriendly neighbors. They gathered reserves that summer, and so did the new baby. He did not spend any time in a clinic, among strangers, but from the first moment of his life came right into the midst of the family, claiming at once his membership in the household, and a big place in everybody's heart. Just at that time there were no air

raids in the city, where my husband worked, and re-
leased from the strain of constant anxiety, I too, had my
perfect time of peace. I lay in the room which I had
once shared with my sister. The windows opened wide
onto the garden, and I could see the trees that had
watched over my childhood—hear from the lawn the
laughter of my own children. No hospital smells, no
troublesome visitors, only the golden stillness of a rich,
ripe season, the sense of perfection and of fulfillment. It
lasted for many days, two or three weeks, in fact; then
war reached us. But meanwhile, the baby put on weight,
and I built up a stock of courage.

Trouble struck in the night, with the menacing roar
of planes going and coming overhead, and "Stalin
candles" and bombs, thrown on the surrounding towns,
illuminating the village. In our respite from attacks
people sat on the benches in front of their houses, filled
with awe, and talked about the end of the world. The
attacks continued, and then one day we were occupied.
A German major came to live in our house. He was an
elderly Austrian, whom we hardly ever saw. He and his
men built bridges on the river, about eight miles from
us, and were away all day. The village lived as before,
except for the illuminated nights.

But one day another detachment of troops arrived.
They came with tanks and wore the emblem of a skull
on their caps. My mother and sister had left home a few
days before, my brother was back in the Service, so the
soldiers came to me to ask permission to use our yard
and stables. I refused it. Next morning the road was
torn up by tanks, and the yard was full of soldiers, going
in and out of the stables. I sent a note of protest to their
officer, but in vain. In the evening I spoke to our

major; I thought perhaps he could help. But he could not. "With these troops there is nothing to do," he said, "they take what they want. I am going to change my quarters, for I do not like to be close to them. But don't think of leaving. A battlefield is no place for women and children."

It was then that I understood that we were really in danger. My husband had already suggested taking us back to town, but I did not want to go. Now I could hardly wait for his coming, I was so anxious to talk things over with him. He came in a few days, and we decided to go home. He was to go back next day and would return to fetch us with a car. But the situation changed during the night. Russian tanks reached the river and the Germans, those from our yard too, went to meet them. My husband would not leave us; he tried to telephone for the car, but no long-distance calls went through. He tried to send a messenger to Budapest, but the man returned two days later; he could not get there; the trains were reserved for soldiers, and the roads were jammed with cars and carriages. We tried to get a car, thought of going with a carriage, made plans for facing a battle, a Russian occupation. For the first time we felt that it was not on our decision alone that our fate depended, we had to wait for God's decision. Whatever this should be, we wanted to accept it with full confidence.

It was in this spirit that I prepared to go to bed one night. While I was changing the baby, there was a knock at the door. It was the major's man, bringing a note. He waited for the answer. "One of my trucks goes tomorrow morning via Budapest," the note read. "You can go with it, if you want to, and may take some luggage." Our decision was thus made for us, and we started to pack.

It was heartbreaking to leave the Old Place, and heart-breaking to see what seemed to be the entire country on the high road; carriages, covered wagons, herds of cattle and horses, flocks of sheep. But otherwise, it was an easy journey, much better than we had dared to hope, and we reached the city before dark. When saying good-bye to the good-humored Viennese soldier who was our driver, I asked, without being really interested: "Where are you going now?" To my surprise he named a village in the western part of the country, and my husband said at once: "Do write a note to Elise." For this was the village where our old cook lived. I scribbled a note, and the driver promised to deliver it. A few days later, on his way back, he brought an answer. Elise urged us to come and stay with her. She could give us a room, there was plenty of food in the village and comparative peace. But at that time we did not think of leaving our home. We still believed that Budapest would be an "open city" with elite troops in charge of the occupation, accompanied by Americans and Britons.

We believed—or rather, hoped—this for three night-marish weeks, during which we lived under the heart-less rule of the alarm sirens. They would blow just as I put the baby into his bath; as I was trying to cook a meal; at the moment the children laid their weary heads on their pillows. Each time we had to run across the street into a shelter, because our cellar was not safe. The maids had gone home to their families, but a friend came to help me. We worked out a plan to get the children dressed in the shortest possible time, and rush them into the shelter. There we had to face the hostile glances of the established occupants. For them we were intruders who had no right to consume their oxygen. Each word, each movement of the children, aroused indignation: these cost oxygen. Finally we had to go to another shelter, which was not so well-built, but where the occupants accepted us. (Later we heard that the first one had got a direct hit, and many of the people were killed.)

The question of the shelter was settled, but there was the even bigger problem of food. We had provisions, but never a chance to prepare a meal. And no milk at all. We lived on bacon and cookies, sometimes a quickly warmed vegetable, a cup of tea. This could not go on much longer. We began to think of going to Elise. When we woke one morning to the sound of guns, and heard that the Regent had left and the new Government was ready to sacrifice the capital, we decided to go.

Some friends wanted to dissuade me from leaving. "Just one or two weeks, then it will surely be over," they said. "Remember how many civilians survived in Stalingrad." But two weeks were a long time for a baby, and how many children had died in Stalingrad? We had to go. We packed again, now with the painful thought that we were probably giving up our home for good. But the children were more important. They, of course, enjoyed the new trip, made this time in a butcher's truck: he was going to the country to buy pigs. We passed Saint Marguerite's bridge a few hours after it was blown up and saw this first deep wound in our city.

Late that day we arrived at Elise's tiny house. There were only two rooms in it: one for her and her three daughters, one for us, and between the two, the kitchen. It was, of course, far from the comfort of our home, or the spacious beauty of the Old Place, but to put our children to bed with the knowledge that they would sleep undisturbed made up for everything. My husband returned to the city, relieved of a great burden.

There was no running water, no electric current in the little house, but I soon learned to fetch water from the well, to light the fire in the iron stove, to clean the oil lamps. In the evening, when the children were fast asleep after a busy day spent in the small garden or in the cornfield, I sat with Elise and her two elder daughters in the kitchen by the oil lamp. The two young girls were cheerful, their mother had a smiling serenity which never left her, not even when we spoke about the immediate future. She had a perfect confidence in God's providence. Was not the fact that we had come to stay with her and provided her with fuel and food for the winter and warm clothing for the girls—all things that had cost her sleepless nights—a new proof of it? She taught me many things about the simple, self-reliant life of the poor, things which I was glad to know when we became of the very poorest. We had been mistress and servant once and had liked each other; now we were friends.

When the girls went to bed, we tried to plan what we should do when the Russians came. The young girls would have to be hidden, and we and the children had better hide too, in the first days. This was a vine-growing country. The cellars of the rich peasants were full of excellent wine, and we had already learned that this was a great danger. The mildest Russian becomes wild when he is drunk. But every hiding-place we thought of: the little wood, the corn-fields, the ravine covered with blackberry brambles, seemed useless in winter. In the house itself there was neither cellar nor attic. Slowly it became clear to me that we could not face a siege here.

But where should we go? Fugitives from the Eastern counties came to the village. Some wanted to go to the Austrian frontier and wait there until the armistice. "Surely they won't fight through the whole country," they speculated. Others wanted to go to Budapest: "It is easier to face it in a big town." I could not figure out what to do. I knew already that a besieged Budapest was no place for the children and feared that the imminent dangers of war would not stop at the frontier. But what lay behind the frontier? Air raids, concentration camps. And what was on the other side of the firing-line which already included the Old Place? Persecution, violation, Communism as we remembered it from 1919. It was like watching fire spreading on every side, and wanting to run away, and knowing not which way to turn. Elise's house was a safe spot so far—but for how long? One evening, as we sat by the oil lamp, one of the girls opened the window and listened: what was this? I recognized the sound, for I had heard it in the Old Place and in Budapest too, in our last days there: the distant rumble and thud of big guns. We went out into the street, and there we heard it more distinctly. All at once, the whole village was awake. People stood in front of their houses, excited, shivering and frightened, as they used to at home when Stalin candles illuminated the night. "What shall we do?" asked the girls. "We shall pray," answered their mother, "and God will give us good advice."

Next day was a First Friday. I went to Mass, and when I came back Elise had a plan already made. She was going to send the elder girls to her brother, who was a gamekeeper. This seemed a good solution. We learned later that it really was. The gamekeeper was well known to be a poor man with no family, so the Russians were not interested in him. If, by some chance, a few stragglers found their way to the house, the gamekeeper hid the girls in the chimney. He hung them up in a kind of hammock.

But Elise was worried about me and the children. I told her I was sure that something would soon turn up, and began to re-pack our luggage. In the evening everything was ready for a move, and I was not at all astonished when my husband woke me in the middle of the night. He had come to fetch us, we had to go at once. He had been ordered to leave the city with the evacuated factory and had obtained permission to take us with him. He could hardly believe me when I explained that I had already packed, and wondered how in the world Elise and I could have guessed he was coming.

We went to a village close to the Austrian border and got a room in a big house owned by a peasant. Its owner, an old woman, was not pleased to see us. She did not want so many children about. "My beautiful room, it will be ruined," she kept on saying; "I am too old to have so much noise, so many people in my house." I was scared and unhappy. It was the first time I had been unwelcome in anyone's house. I sat down to feed the baby, very near to tears; my husband heroically took over the task of making all arrangements with the old woman, who was still complaining. But when I went to the kitchen later, I found her sitting by the stove, telling a fairy tale to her grandson, whose blackhaired little head lay in her lap, and beside it, just as confidently, was the fair, curled one of my three-year-old. The old woman stroked both little heads and smiled at me: "Is he not a darling?" she said. "He likes me already." Very soon we all liked her, and she us—we called her "Aunt."

The village was incredibly crowded. Soldiers slept in the stables, refugees in the barns; people started to rent beds or mattresses in the corner of the kitchen, or in the enviable privacy of a pantry. Because of the continuous traffic the mud was knee-deep on the road. Fortunately, we lived at the end of the village and could walk straight out to the meadows. One sunny morning, when snow covered the mud, we went into the village. We passed the little convent, an enchanted island of peace in the middle of all the military traffic. The nuns were just coming out, wearing big white aprons. They crossed the street, marching in a line with careful steps, carrying cakes and pies to the baker. The whole street seemed to stop and watch them, and one or the other weary soldier sighed: "They are preparing for Christmas. What a Christmas for us again!" The children caught up the word Christmas. "Will it soon be Christmas, really?" The two big ones spoke excitedly about the big tree and all the toys they had had the year before. "You do not remember," they told their little brother, "but you will see. And Baby, how surprised he will be!" I did not know how to tell them that it would not be at all like last year, and let them talk until we reached the church. We went in to say a prayer to Little Jesus, who sends Christmas presents to children, and there we saw a picture of Him: the Flight into Egypt. On our way back I had to tell the children all about it. They opened wide, wondering eyes, and the voice of the youngest rang out like a tiny silver bell: "Was Bethlehem bombarded? Did Little Jesus have to go away like us?" "Yes," I said, "He too had to leave at night, all of a sudden, but they could not take so many things, they had only the little donkey, no truck. There were no toys for Little Jesus, and no warm room, like the one we have with Aunt." After this we prepared for Christmas by talking about these things every evening and praying to Little Jesus to show us the way to Nazareth.

One night I went to the convent to ask the sisters if they had any toys. They had none left, but they still had cardboard, paper and paints, and with these they made dolls and teddy bears for each child. And they gave me some colored paper, too, to decorate the tree. I hid these treasures in my jewel-box—I still had it then but lost it later on our next move—and on Christmas Eve, while the children were playing in Aunt's room, we decorated the little tree and put the paper figures under it. I had real stage fright: What will the children say, the two big ones, who remember last Christmas? Will they be disappointed? Then they came in; I watched them with the baby in my arms. Their eyes shone like stars, they sang the little song we had taught them, and then the eldest boy exclaimed: "This is the most beautiful tree we ever had," and the little girl clasped her paper doll and cried: "Look, we even have toys!" Little Jesus had given them the gift of contentment—the key to happiness.

We prayed to get to Nazareth, but we were not even in Egypt yet. We had to go to the lake district with the personnel and machines belonging to the factory. But we had difficulties. The first evacuation train left without us and so did the next one. There was always some obstacle: the children were ill, our papers were not in order. The whole winter passed and we were still in Aunt's house. In the evenings she sat with us, told fairy tales to the children, admired the baby and taught me how to knit stockings. We did not like to think of our departure, but one day it had to come. We left one morning, and that very evening the attack started. Aunt and her family survived it, though the house—and the room where we lived—was hit several times.

When we arrived at our destination—dead-tired and without my jewels—we thanked God for having kept us in that village until the last moment. Things were very bad in Austria. There were several hundred persons crowded into one big factory room, as if we were as lifeless as the machines among and under which we slept on straw. Our bath was the ice-cold mountain stream, our kitchen a fire between two stones. When at long last we found a room, it was only to receive the "Gauleiter's" order to leave the town and go to a camp, in what was to become the Russian Zone. We tried to avoid this by procuring a permit to join my sister in the Western Alps. No one could travel without a permit, although the trains were still going regularly. Day after day my husband went to ask for this permit and was refused, until at last he found an official who had a heart and gave it to him. Then we reduced our luggage to the minimum and took the train.

Normally it would have been a journey of twenty-four hours, but this time it lasted five days. We had to change trains several times and were often left behind. It was not easy to get onto these crowded trains with four small children and our luggage. The first night we slept out of doors; the next night we felt we were in heaven in the dry corner of an old coach, while the rain was pouring in the other corner. Once we tried to find shelter in a Nazi hospice, but the nurse there refused to give us a bed and milk for the baby, because we were unwanted foreigners. When at last we arrived in the little town where my sister lived then, the baby was half starved and very sick. Here again we could not get permission to stay, but our landlord was touched by the sick child and kept us illegally.

The baby's illness made us stay in that beautiful place, which was to be our Egypt for the following five years. Materially these were difficult years, but we learned not to worry. Help always came in time, and generally in some most unexpected way. Each day had its little miracle. Once, when food was very scarce, a young woman knocked at our door with four loaves of white bread: a real treasure then. She was the baker's wife and wanted to learn French—would I give her lessons for bread and flour? Later, when the children needed winter coats and the shops were still all closed, I went to the tailor whom I knew to be a good Catholic. I asked him to make coats for my children, offering to pay whatever he asked. (This was before the devaluation, and we still had money.) He refused, saying he had no time. I did not try the other tailor, who was a reputed Nazi and who I knew was very busy. But a few days later his wife came to me. She knew the children and noticed that they needed warm clothing. She said her husband could make coats for them out of some remnants he had—would I like that? He did make them and refused to accept anything in return except my tobacco ration.

Later on parcels came from dear friends in the U.S.A. and Switzerland. They always seemed to know exactly what we needed, and when we needed it most. And somehow—this was the greatest miracle—we always found some work, we could always keep a small apartment and give the children a home. It was a very poor home, but we were happy in it, and all day long the wonderful scenery of this Alpine paradise belonged to the children.

But all this was transitory. It was not Nazareth yet.

Where should we find it? Not in our own country, alas, and this not because our home had been burned down and the Old Place taken bit by bit, field after field and room after room from the family, but because of the children. We could not expose them to the dangers of a determinedly anti-Christian education. We had to take them somewhere else. But where? It was not easy to go to a foreign country with four children and no means. Then my sister and her family came to the U.S.A. to their relatives. They found sponsors for us, and through the generous help of the N.C.W.C. we were soon on our way.

Beginning a new life is difficult, of course. But the knowledge that God's providence brought us here gives us confidence and strength. People are so kind that one cannot feel lonely, and there is another thing. Yesterday, I took a walk with the children and we came to the river. We stopped to admire it as it wound red with the sunset, into the misty darkness of the horizon. "What river is this?" asked the children. "The Delaware," I said. This name brought back the taste of the small, thick-skinned red grapes I used to pick as a child from the side of the old arbor, and which my children had picked from the old vinestock during that last summer at home. A straight line seemed to lead from the Old Place to this American river.

Oh, Lord, let us always recognize the lines you draw for us.

OUR CHILD IS MENTALLY DEFECTIVE

ANONYMOUS

THE PRESENCE OF EVIL in the universe of an All-Good, All-Powerful Creator is more than an academic challenge when it confronts you, the Man in the Street. A solution becomes an urgent personal necessity. You cry, with Saint Augustine: "Whence is this evil?"

When the doctor told us that our baby was mentally defective, our reaction was one of incredulity. Surely he—only a country practitioner, after all—had made a mistake. It wasn't possible that we were the victims of this Thing that happens, the doctor said, only once in ten thousand times.

We left his office to begin the long pursuit of the will-o'-the-wisp of hope. It beckoned us into the office of an ear specialist—perhaps the child was only deaf. "Just deaf" would be infinitely better than the other. It led us into the modernistic salon of a Park Avenue bio-chemist. He told us nothing at ten dollars a minute for five minutes. Perhaps we ought to see a brain man, we thought next. Thus hope teased us along a path of cruel self-delusion for many months. Like tenderfoots lost in the forest, we came back to where we'd started—and we were still lost.

My husband began to avoid the company of the child. He never went into the nursery, and he made it plain that any conversations on the subject were painful. I began to dramatize myself as a valiant figure, fighting this battle nobly and alone. I am ashamed to admit that I even did my husband the injustice of considering him callous and unfeeling. Fathers want to be proud of their sons. They take them fishing and watch them play football; a father's loving folly prompts him to buy an electric train long before the little fellow is old enough to know the difference between a transformer and a caboose. My husband's grief was inarticulate. His only armor was to act the role of tough guy. From the perspective of time, I see now that I was far from alone in this desolate period.

Our son was two years old when Mary was born. She came into the world, charming and alert from the moment she filled her lungs with the alien Connecticut air and started squalling. Every day the difference between the two children became more marked as Mary followed the normal pattern of development. She outstripped her brother in only a few weeks.

The time had come. We could no longer ignore the truth of the situation that no human agency could make whole the congenitally defective son whom we had brought into the world with expectation and joy. We had to go on from there.

Our prayers bombarded Heaven. We had Masses said and the Sisters made innumerable novenas. God works miracles all the time, we reassured ourselves. I remember spending hour after hour trying to teach our son, whispering just once more, "Little Flower, make him do it, make him do it, this simple little gesture!" But he never learned to do it.

Time mitigated the shock, but the heaviness of heart grew that comes with living with sorrow intimately, month after interminable, unrelieved month. Our emotions were spent. Psychologically this was the most crucial phase of our readjustment. For it was then that we were tempted to question the Will of God. Perhaps we were no more than His pawns in the pastime of Eternity. Omar's philosophy was hateful but specious. Why had the hand of the Potter shaken as he scooped up the primeval clay, imprisoning an immortal soul in the imperfect vase of our child's body? Was He a sadistic god, using power in the manner of an Infinite Bully? These thoughts came to me many times as I watched the little boy with the aureole of golden hair. They came, unbidden, during the night when his constant wailing filled me with the sense of indescribable desolation that Matthew Arnold called "the eternal note of human sadness." I thought beyond this present and personal grief and saw it as only a microcosm in the tide of war, disease, corruption and sin that engulfs all mortal things. That I had company in my sorrow did not alleviate the misery. It served rather to enhance it. I was aware of its universal implications.

I discussed these thoughts with my confessor. He told me that God would send me the grace I needed, that even Our Lord had cried, "My God, My God, why hast Thou forsaken Me?"

Our second child was very ill during the first days following her birth. This precipitated a decision to which we had been reluctant to bring ourselves. We placed our

I

son in the care of a woman whose name you would not recognize but whose work on behalf of a small group of defective children has been heroic. She was a trained nurse. She had abandoned an easier phase of her profession from concern over the lack of facilities for the care of these children and had opened a twenty-bed hospital. When I took our son to place him there, she took me into the ward. As I looked at the monstrous infants in the little white beds, I said to her, "How sad this all is—they would be so lovely if they were normal!"

Her answer was vehement. Stroking the head of a tiny hydrocephalic baby, she replied passionately, "They are lovely—otherwise God would not have made them!"

Her fee was ridiculously low, and she never asked parents to pay for extra items, such as oxygen and special medications and doctors' consultations. Our association with her was an important factor in our recovery from the emotional and spiritual damage we had undergone. She had opened a door!

Our child has never come home again. We believe that the care he is getting now is far better than any we could provide, and that his presence would prejudice the psychological welfare of the three little daughters who are entitled to a normal home. We seldom talk about our son, and we visit him only when an emergency makes it advisable. This required at first a degree of self-discipline on our part. It appears, for us, the wiser course. Conforming to it has become automatic. Only once in a while do I remember, as is written in *Kristin Lavransdatter*, that a mother's heart is never delivered of its burden as the womb is.

After fifteen years of trial-and-error groping for the answer to Saint Augustine's "Whence is this evil?", we have found the answer.

And the answer surprised us. What we thought evil was in reality a manifestation of God's goodness. Our prayers have been answered—and far more generously than we had dared hope in the days we prayed for a miracle.

This experience has brought us from shallowness and doubt to the deeper, unsounded waters of spiritual understanding and human sympathy. It has not made saints of us—we are too blamed ornery for that—but we hope that it has purified our lives of much that was superficial and worldly. God has given us a precious commodity, the gift of interior peace that comes with unconcern for the ephemeral and the temporal. He has honored us with a privilege, for we have been the vessel in which has been raised to Him a soul utterly uninfected by the contagion of sin. Our son's life has been a constant act of reparation for the irreligion and materialism of the world in which he will never move.

Besides these spiritual blessings, God has provided temporal blessings with splendid largesse, making us sensitive to His Face in the stars and seas and the panorama of the seasons. He has increased our capacity for joy in the three little rosy-cheeked daughters who get A's on their report cards and are sometimes remiss in washing behind their ears. This life looks good to us.

I believe that our mentally defective child has justified his existence in time as well as in eternity. The investment of mortal tears will return immortal dividends.

Saint Paul wrote: "Our own tribulation which is at present momentary and light worketh for us above measure exceedingly an eternal weight of glory."

What more can we ask?

THE YOUNG FAMILIAR FACES

ɔ⊷ɔ

WILLIAM WALSH

Bill was sitting, surrounded by ashtrays (full) and coffee cups (empty), in Saliman's Grill in downtown Denver. It was the summer of 1950, when he was finishing work on his Ph.D. Avis sat across the booth from him, as usual, sometimes taking dictation in a stenographer's note book and sometimes listing vocabulary for him to study. It had been a torch of a summer. But it was cool here in the Grill, and Bill and Avis could fight sleep with coffee. They could work in the park all right in the mornings, but in the afternoons no one can stay awake in a summer park—except children, of course. And Avis and Bill were not children any more—they were thirty-eight years old, and they both felt their combined ages along about midafternoon. They had been averaging nearly twenty hours a day of galling work for the last year and a half. And besides earning a living, Bill still had his French finals to take over again, the dissertation to polish up, and his orals still to accomplish. There was barely a month left in which to focus all these things.

Bill pushed the five-hundred-page dissertation to one

side of the long, littered table. He had spent his allotted time for one day on this particular phase of his work, so he reached for the French vocabulary Avis had been preparing for him. He studied it intensely for fifteen minutes, then handed the page back and began to write. He missed on the three last words out of the fifty, almost sobbing as he got to the end of the list. He was pretty tired.

"Let's have another cup of coffee," Avis said. "It's getting kind of drowsy in here."

They began looking around for their usual waitress— a little Italian girl with four kids who sometimes put coffee and sandwiches "on the cuff" for them till Saturday. She was nowhere in sight, but the hard-looking blonde was plainly visible to them three booths away, sneaking a cigarette over by the window. This wasn't her side of the Grill, and as a matter of fact, this section was always closed in the afternoon, except to Bill and Avis.

For four years they had been coming here at odd times to study. The proprietor was not, like Bill, a family man, nor Irish, nor Catholic. He was not even a Christian. But he had told them they could come any time they wanted to and stay as long as they liked, and if anybody told them to leave, they were just to call for him.

Besides charity, the proprietor had also the virtue of artistry with food: Saliman's roast beef sandwiches on pumpernickel served with green peppers (or horseradish or dill pickles, as Avis sometimes preferred) are the best food in the world. The Walshes paid two-bits for their sandwiches and five cents a cup for coffee (it was nearly a year after the fact before they learned from a new waitress that the prices had actually gone up to thirty-five and ten).

The blonde waitress stood staring hard into the July afternoon street, puffing her cigarette and muttering to herself.

"How about some coffee?" Bill called to her pleasantly. But she didn't seem to hear him. She was watching the street like a secret agent.

"Damn it all," she said finally, grinding out her cigarette savagely. "There they go again." She moved, frowning, towards the booth where Avis and Bill sat waiting. "You ought to take a gander out into that street," she said, disgustedly. "One of them punks is gonna be hamburger pretty soon."

Glad to stand up and stretch, they peered idly over the walled booth into the heat-glazed street. Traffic zoomed along as usual, making a kaleidoscopic glare on sun-reflecting glass and metal; street cars rumbled and clanged along and big busses ground out noise and passengers. They didn't see anything unusual about the familiar afternoon street. And then the nearest bus lurched out of the way and they did see—the children!

There were three little kids right out in the middle of the street fighting the traffic down towards the center of the block. They all looked under five years old. On the opposite curb stood a slender woman with a baby in her arms. She was gesturing frantically to the children.

Avis was out of the Grill, with Bill at her heels, so quickly that they were both momentarily blinded by the sun. They bumped into people as they ran, and evidently Bill wasn't speaking French now because the people got out of the way without argument. When their eyes became accustomed to the glare, Avis and

Bill could see the children still in midstream, and the passing cars were honking angrily at them but not slowing down. First one and then the other of the kids would try to dart between the moving cars. Just as Avis and Bill reached the curb opposite the frantic mother, one of the children leapt between two almost bumper-to-bumper cars, and made it to the curb, but the other two had not been quick enough.

The two-way traffic slowed accidentally for a few seconds while a truck made a turn at the corner, and in this pause Avis and Bill fought their way to the children, Bill banging his fist on fenders and radiators, and Avis addressing scornful diatribes to the unheeding drivers. They gathered the children up in their arms and held them high as they waded to the opposite curb. It was a ridiculously dramatic performance, but it worked.

They got the children to safety, and did not feel at all like heroes.

The mother of the little towheads cried and swore alternately at the traffic and the kids. But she pulled herself together quickly, thanked Avis and Bill, and started off up the street with her little family marching nonchalantly in front of her. Avis and Bill watched them plunge again into the traffic at the cross-street, shook their heads sadly, and went back to the cool of Saliman's.

The blonde was still standing by their table. Her face was still hard and cynical, but there were now two fresh cups of black coffee on the newly wiped table. They dropped, shaking a little, into their accustomed places, and Bill lit a new cigarette off the old one, and dropped the old one into the recently emptied tray.

"Well, you got the traffic stopped, that's something," the blonde said with a wry smile. "But it won't do any good—they'll be right back where they started again in five minutes. They're from the Tennessee hills."

"How the hell do you know?" Bill said, still angry from the traffic. "And what do you mean it won't do any good? They aren't dead yet, anyway."

The waitress perched her nice young body on a table opposite the Walshes' booth. Her hard face and nice body and throaty voice all seemed to belong in a Humphrey Bogart movie. "No, but they will be," she said, "if somebody don't do somethin'."

"Why don't *you* do something?" Avis said, and then apologized. She was still pretty sad, too—and tired with the sudden force of reaction.

The blonde lit another of her long cigarettes, took a few quick puffs and crushed it out. That's the way she always smoked. "I did what I could," she said in that emotionless voice of hers. "I've fed 'em four times in the last two days out of my wages, but I can't shag 'em up and down the street, and if I took 'em to my apartment there would be hell to pay."

Avis and Bill looked at each other, embarrassed—with that very special embarrassment one always feels in the presence of good people one has underestimated. Avis recovered first and asked, "Why didn't you tell us they were in need? We still have a roof over our heads, and we'd gladly share it with them. I don't know what, or how, we'd feed them, but we'd be willing to try."

The waitress looked at them quietly. "You can't do it. I know more about you than you think I do—you've got a dozen kids of your own and most of them are little. I come from a big family myself—my father was a back-country preacher. Us kids never had a damn thing of our own, and I wouldn't shove any more of that kind of a life onto your kids than they've got already."

"Well," Bill said, "you seem to have come through all right. If you'd been chronically undernourished you wouldn't be built like you are now."

"I ran away from home when I was thirteen," she replied thoughtfully. "I'll never go back. I send money home for the kids, but if God doesn't like the way I get it, that's just too bad."

Avis and Bill both more or less knew the blonde's "reputation"—that is, they knew from hearsay the evil side only.

"For the last three days," the hard young face was saying, "that Tennessee hill girl and her four kids have been wandering around this town trying to raise the price of food in the daytime, and they've been sleeping in the park at night. I've seen fat business men right here in this restaurant snarl at that girl for asking for two-bits for her kids. And I've seen other greasy bastards try to make a date with her—no date, no money. If she didn't have a husband she might get charity in a month or so. Her husband can't find work, they're from out of State, they're broke, and that's all there is to it. Who cares? If God does, He isn't letting them know it."

"Well, He sent them to you—" Bill began. But the girl was gone. She had to get back to work.

Avis and Bill did what they could. They left their things in the Grill and went looking for the woman and the kids. It took a long time to find them. When they finally located the little troupe they took them to the Y.W.C.A. because it was next to Saliman's and they wanted to get the children bathed while Bill got food for them.

While Bill went back to his briefcase to get some of his books to sell, Avis stayed with the woman and kids— bathed the two biggest of the children, talked to the

woman, gave her their address and directions how to get
to the Walsh house after she had met her husband at
their appointed park bench that evening.

When Bill came back to the Y.W., sandwiches in his
hands, to wait for them, he ran into the young friend
of his, Howard Farrand, a recent convert, whose orches-
tra was to have a one-night dance job at the place that
same evening. Howard listened to the story of the Tennessee strays, gave Bill five dollars, went immediately
to the phone booth and called all the charity organizations in town. The organizations all passed the buck,
but he finally lined up a place for them to sleep that
night if the woman's husband objected to going ten
miles out into the suburbs to stay with the Walshes.

When the woman and her four children and Avis
finally joined Bill and Howard in the lobby, the two
men explained the tentative arrangements, and Avis
further arranged a place for the woman's husband to
meet them the next day, in case none of the present
suggestions fitted his plans. Bill then gave the woman
what money he had left. They all left the Y.W. together,
and the last Avis and Bill saw of the woman and kids
they were heading down Fifteenth Street for the grocery
store.

Howard went back to Saliman's with Avis and Bill
for a chat and coffee. They talked of the woman and
her kids a little and then Howard left. Bill glanced at
the clock and started sorting through his papers. He was
an hour behind schedule. With a prayer he dismissed
the last hour from his mind—there had been nothing
very unusual about the woman's story, nor about what
they had done about it, and it was so typical of the life
they'd led these twenty years that it did not throw

Bill's work off-stride. Things like that happen all over the country every hour of the day and night—all over the world, for that matter. If the poor didn't help each other, the human race would have been out of business centuries ago.

Bill picked up his dissertation again where he had left off re-writing, and went back to work on it. Avis began listing vocabulary for tomorrow's Chaucer class. It was near evening now, and Saliman's was filling up. They'd have to shove off pretty soon and go home to their own twelve children. Bill glanced again at the clock. "It's nearly six o'clock," he said to Avis. "We ought to start home by seven."

"We'd better have a sandwich first," she answered, and then, a bit too casually, she said, "I wonder where *our* waitress is today—we haven't had anything but coffee since early this morning."

Bill ordered two roast beef sandwiches, and two more black coffees from one of the newer waitresses—one they didn't know. Then they both bent intently over their work, and when Bill finally glanced up at the clock again it was six-forty-five and the sandwiches and coffee had not come. As though by mutual consent they started to talk about the blonde waitress. She had been at the back of their thoughts all the time. They had known, across the years, many people like her. "They are the hardest people to really reach," Avis said sadly. "Yes," Bill agreed, "because they know about God but they do not love Him, and they hate injustice but they do not love justice, and they hate meanness, but they do not love the practice of charity." He was about to enlarge on the familiar theme, but he saw his wife's lips moving in silent prayer, so he too fell silent.

The noise of the dinner-time Grill was at concert pitch now—with the banging of dishes, loud, cheerful belly-talk, and over all the juke box howling the untouching lyrics of a rather too touching melody called "Slipping Around." Everybody must have been slipping around that night—the juke box ground out no other melody for the next forty minutes. The sandwiches still had not come, and the new waitress seemed almost hysterical as she charged back and forth with various parts of all the orders she was trying to fill simultaneously. They did not want to add to her sorrows, so they waited patiently.

Avis was sitting very straight with her serene face cupped in her hands. It was now seven o'clock. She had fallen sound asleep. Bill reached into his briefcase for a battered old notebook which, because he did not know what else to call it, he called a journal. This particular notebook was the thirty-sixth volume he had written for his private perusal in the hoped-for calm of old age. He read a couple of the previous entries, made the Sign of the Cross, picked up his pen and began to write:

A man cannot with impunity carry on a flirtation with God. If ever, once only, in the deep quiet of his most secret heart he says to God, "I love You," he is immediately wedded to a creative force so virile, so passionate, that his whole being is at once impregnated. He feels himself growing mis-shapen with new life—and yet glad with a strange gladness. No matter how his condition moves others to false pity or stupid laughter, he *knows* that in time he will be delivered of some form of life that God wants born into the world.

Sometimes a man who has spoken the words of consent to God becomes afterwards terrified at the manifestation in himself of His creative vigor. If, however, instead of fearful submission, he puts down his foolish terror, at that moment of free reciprocal love there is instigated in his behalf the protective tenderness that we have learned to call the providence of God. It is the gift bestowed on those who love freely and therefore are said to trust God.

But it is the protective tenderness of the good husband, and it is not without sternness. Its sweetness is in its strangely unpredictable constancy, not in the idle satisfaction of every whim of the recipient—and like all perfect gifts it always involves surprise. Perhaps God Himself is always a little surprised by a man's free love, and so (since He will not be outdone), He shows the man a little of the giant value God places on freedom! He gives freedom itself in each of His gifts to the man who loves freely. Grace is the first, and greatest, of His gifts. It is alone sufficient. And because it is sufficient He sometimes gives nothing else at all, not even in emergencies. Sometimes He gives much else. But if the loving man falters in his love, then he may get lesser gifts on demand, perhaps to shame him, as a father will sometimes give an impatient child a penny sucker when he was going to take him farther along the street to buy him a banana split. Grace, through Christ's life, death, and resurrection, cancels the curse of Eden and *allows* a man to grow, to expand, through understood pain, and so to love even more freely and so to work patiently toward the great task of *perfecting* his love.

The little gifts of food, clothing, and shelter, position, friends, the quiet mind, are nothing to the gift of grace itself, for in *that* gift man receives the capacity to love with Christ's own love—

The wrong kind of impatience is a danger, but the great danger is in a man's temptation to bargain with God—

Avis came awake with a start as the blonde waitress put down the sandwiches and coffee in front of them on the table. Bill hurriedly slapped his journal shut and tucked it out of sight in his huge briefcase. They had not ordered the sandwiches from the blonde because, of course, this was not her side of the Grill. And they could not see her station from their booth, and she could not see them. Yet she brought them food.

"I'm off duty now," she said. "The new girl's got her orders all mixed up, so I figured you probably haven't eaten yet." She was gone before they could thank her or pay for the food.

The rich light of evening was in the streets as they walked down Fifteenth toward the Interurban station. It was seven-thirty now, and the streets were empty with that waiting emptiness of cities between homeward hurry after the closing of stores and the slow beginning of the night life of the place. In summer this period is a long one. The streets this evening were cool and smilingly quiet. As Avis and Bill walked along they could see the distant mountains beyond the ends of many streets, and the trees and fields under a green-gold sky between the mountains and the town. High clouds underlit by rose from beyond the hills rode serenely in the untroubled bay of the day.

The 84 Interurban left the loop at five minutes after each hour, and Bill and Avis always gave themselves half an hour to saunter down from Saliman's. The resting town was pleasant to them at this hour in a very special way. They were resting, too. One shift was over for them, and another would not begin for at least an hour. They would ride out now into the green suburbs, get supper, talk and read to the kids, get the littlest children off to bed, put on a fresh pot of coffee, and then buckle down again to the night shift of study. This evening interval of pause was therefore infinitely precious to them—and the long relaxing ride out through the rising countryside always restored their souls, and the thought of going home again was forever wonderful with remembered accomplishment, with waiting affection, and with promise.

Although it had been a hot day, they carried coats over their arms, and Bill carried his huge briefcase, while Avis swung the squeaky little portable typewriter to sort of balance her huge pocketbook. It was always necessary to carry a coat in Denver if you were going to be away from home for any length of time—rainstorms come and go in the mountain country in the summer, and besides, the Walshes often worked in one of the parks or on the Civic Center lawn where a spread-out coat somehow staked off a private world and discouraged ants. Of course, people with automobiles do not have to carry armloads of equipment, but Avis and Bill never owned a car except one time for three weeks—but that's another story.

When they arrived at the Interurban station they were fifteen minutes ahead of the car, so they unloaded their paraphernalia on one of the long outside porch benches and sat down to enjoy the cloud-colored quiet.

"By the way," Bill yawned, "you'll have to spot me carfare. I gave every cent I had to that woman with the kids. I even sold some of my books so I wouldn't have to ask you for any of the food money."

Avis sat looking dreamily out at the darkening streets. Bill thought she didn't hear what he said. So he repeated the request. It was an old game with them—they had so little money that they divided it up to make it seem like more and then spent their days borrowing from each other under the illusion that one of them had a fairy godparent who would underwrite the loan. This sort of thing is one of the pleasantries of the poor, as old as time and as universal as hunger.

"Well," she said, "let's face it. I didn't know you were going to sell your books, so I gave her all the food money—"

"What!" Bill fairly screamed. "You mean *all* the food money, for the whole week?"

"Yes," she answered quietly, "the whole fifteen dollars."

"Well, I'll be damned!" Bill said. "Now what are *we* supposed to do? It's ten miles home, and I've got to get to school the rest of the week—every class counts now; and I've got examinations to take—you knew that."

"The kids have got to eat, too," she answered—as though that made the situation better instead of worse.

Well, that did it. They would have to walk. They had walked home before this, of course; and they had walked down, too, carrying boxes of books on their shoulders to sell, so that they could buy groceries and carry them home again to save carfare for the next school day. But you waste whole days doing things like that, and Bill didn't have any more days to waste with the finals coming up so soon.

"Maybe," Avis remarked hopefully, "the Interurban conductor will be one of the men we know—he'll trust us, won't he?"

"If we know him; and if we've paid him for the last time, maybe he will," Bill responded glumly.

But when the huge yellow 84 rumbled around the corner to the stop in front of the station they both knew it was no use asking. This particular genius of transportation had reminded them often enough that the Denver and Intermountain Railway Corporation wasn't run on credit, and it hadn't helped when Bill had answered, a bit too sharply, "No, nor on time, either."

So they picked up their equipage (that's the French word for an overload as far as footsoldiers are concerned) and headed off toward the West. It was an uphill march all the way. Lakewood is more or less in the foothills above the town, and the Walsh house was ten miles as the crow flies from this Interurban station. They knew it would be around midnight before they could get home, and even if they had had a nickel there was no use phoning the kids to go ahead with supper unless David had been lucky enough to pick up a couple of dollars caddying. But if he was still caddying the tournament, which they knew he was, he wouldn't get paid until the end of the week.

"Well," Avis mused as they trudged along in the old Larimer Street section, "Rene has orders to break into the 'reserve supply' if we're not home by eight-thirty." (The "reserve supply" consisted of a ten-pound bag of rice, a large loaf of French bread, and two cans of milk.) They felt easier in their minds, considering how fortunate they were to have this reserve supply. Of course it would only take care of one meal now, because it had been twice broken into lately and the rice was about two-thirds gone, but they had put back the two cans of milk and the French bread, and screwed the hinges back on the cabinet. The huge lock on the cabinet only deceived the littlest kids—all the larger ones knew the hinges could be removed by pulling out the hinge-pins.

"They'll have their supper, anyway," Bill reasoned, "but I'll have to knock off tomorrow and sell more books,

K

and then I'll have to arrange to take the tests next week."

They walked on in silence, mile after uphill mile. There was no use stopping because there was no place to sit down. This is simply not a pedestrian's world. They would rest for a while, they assured each other every few blocks, in the drugstore, at the county line, and if the clerks weren't too busy there, maybe even have a glass of water on the house.

They made the county-line drug store by a little after ten. They were more than half-way home now and doing all right, considering the weighty amount of material they had to carry. They felt hopeful, because the worst of the uphill climb was now behind them. The girl back of the fountain was one of Bill's former students, so they had two glasses of water each, and rested fifteen minutes. They didn't dare rest any longer. Once you cool down completely it's hard (especially at the age of three hundred and thirty-eight or thereabouts) to get rolling again, and they badly needed sleep—months of it. Years of it, really. They couldn't risk dozing off at the soda fountain.

An hour later—or maybe it was a thousand years—they reached Carr Street, the turn-off place from the main road. They would be home now in fifteen minutes. Carr Street was dark except right here at the corner where the brand new business district was lit up like a carnival till midnight. Carr Street was quiet, too, and the road had a different texture. One block past the turnoff, if Carr Street had been marked off by blocks, you are in the country. People go to bed early. The wide-spaced houses sit far back from the street under big trees. The change is so abrupt from the lights and noise and speeding traffic of the main highway that it shocks you, lik stepping through a wall into a hidden garden in a city street.

They had not noticed the moonlight until now because the moon was back of them and because the neon-lighted highway shuts off moonlight more effectively than does a roof. But now they were in the country, in the moonlight, near their own home! Their tired spirits lifted. They could catch glimpses in the distance through the trees of the upstairs light in the little kids' bedroom. The feedsack-curtained and partially boarded window of the room emitted a strange angular light high up, like a lighthouse beacon on a stormy night. They tried to quicken their pace with that unwisdom that makes an eager distance-runner break his stride on the home stretch. When they reached the Interurban tracks, which were halfway between the highway and their home, Bill stumbled and fell full-length with a sort of sliding-into-second twist on the jagged roadway surface.

He stumbled to his feet again, cursing like a madman. He raved and ranted there in the moonlight, lashing out at fate, at circumstance, and even at God's indifference—he had had all he could take—this cruel fall near the end of a hard journey seemed to symbolize to him the diabolical tricks of fate which prevent men, no matter how hard they work, how sincerely they try, how courageously they endure, from final fulfillment.

There would be no point in cataloguing the institutions and events and circumstances against which Bill inveighed with great particularity on this occasion. It is always the same list of things with him, but it always adds up to Mediocrity, against which he works, rather than curses, in his saner hours. The doctor, or priest, or teacher who displays the petty mind—the neighbor who

judges by appearances—the false scale of values in society, etc., etc., etc. Against the mediocrity in himself he
casts his heaviest sarcasm. And it always ends up the
same way, too—in a sort of rage of pain in which the
providence of God is accused of cruel delay.

On this particular occasion, exhausted, overworked,
discouraged, and then presented with the last straw in
the form of the painful fall to the jagged ground, Bill
fixed his attention upon the fact that they had done
everything they could for the woman and the four children, and that they were now completely broke, their
already hungry children about to go hungrier, his long
fight for the Ph.D. jeopardized because he would not
even be able to get to school to take the examinations
and would have to walk the streets trying to sell books
again instead of studying and doing the crucial work
on his unfinished dissertation. He felt trapped, and like
a trapped animal he snarled and roared in anguish at
the empty sky.

Lights began to go on in the neighborhood. Bill had
been making quite a racket. He quieted down, picked
up his things, and started for home, mumbling to himself.

"God has never yet forsaken us," Avis said.

"No," Bill answered. "And in emergency He has never
yet provided for us. He always waits until the pain is
really unendurable, until I come as near to blasphemy
as I did just now. *Why* does He do that? I know He's
going to show His Fatherly care, but I also know that I
can't patiently wait—that I have never been able to wait
patiently. He waits until I make a direct claim against
Him for some specific, immediate necessity, and then
when He actually does help me with the material things
I have already lost the spirit to receive them. In ever

material advantage He has ever given me I seem to have lost by it spiritually. It is an odd way for God to show His providential love for His creatures."

"It is an odd way you have of showing God your love, too," Avis said.

"But He can *afford* to be patient—I can not," Bill cried out. "I've willingly given up much for Him, but I can't give up temperament. When I am wounded, I cry out and I can't help it. I will never be able to help it. And then I justify myself for the weakness and rationalize the whole thing and that spoils everything. I feel empty after He fills me—emptier than before, because empty of Him! It is not despair. It is a physical reaction—physical and psychological, and emotional. It is like the panic I feel when I have dived too deep in a lake—or when I nearly fall off a high mountain cliff. Why does He *wait* to help people who love Him? If they needed His help to prove His existence or to prove His love, or to prove their love for Him, I could understand it. I do not love Him for what He gives me, and He knows that. I would love Him anyway because He is Himself, and I adore Him in the simple splendor of that giant fact. But when I reach the place where life itself becomes an agony to me, and then after blaming myself I turn to Him for the whole thing, He gives me the particular thing I ask for even though He knows it is not the thing I most want—almost out of scorn, it seems to me sometimes. But He knows I do not doubt His existence or His love. He knows that I only want to love Him completely. Then why does He do this to me?"

"Between presumption and despair—" Avis began.

"This has nothing to do with presumption and despair," Bill snapped. "It has to do simply with dignity

—with hating to break down, and knowing I am going to."

"Pride is at the roots of presumption and despair both," Avis trailed off.

They were now at the gate. The house was blazing with light. The children were making much more than their usual nocturnal uproar, especially for so late an hour. When Avis and Bill went into the house they found the children in festive mood. They had been having a party. On Bill's desk, on the piano, the mantel, and the kitchen table, and even on the floor were great earthenware bowls of the kind you see in a hotel kitchen, and many of the bowls were still crammed with food. There were several partly empty bowls on the little library table and there were empty bowls in the sink. Neither Bill nor Avis was particularly amazed, although they should have been, perhaps. Things like this had often happened across the years, but never before exactly on time. Before, the good fortune had always immediately preceded or followed desperation. A little too late, usually—or so it seemed. "Just before despair sets in— and after anguish!" Bill reflected. "But this time right on the nose; the food was here in the house already while I stood out in the road and abused God." He felt terribly empty at first and then strangely at peace.

Rene and David and Gael, talking all at once, told their parents how Mary Marr, one of Bill's special students, had been in charge of a church supper at which there had been too much food, and so she had thought of the Walshes and brought the extra food out to them. "But she needs to have the bowls back," Rene remembered. They told excitedly, too, about the party—and the party, it seemed, had been staged by John Hester and his wife, Helen, and was another affair, entirely separate from the bowls of food. Other friends—Al Lambrecht and his wife, Shirley, and "Skippy" and Don Hibschmann, had dropped in even earlier and brought the children cake and ice-cream, and then taken some of them for a ride. And then later, *after* the party and the bowls of food and the second party and the rides, still other of their friends, headed by Fred Heidemann and Howard Farrand and Bernie Hartmann, had come and waited hours for them, and one of the visitors had left money he owed Bill for books. Gael triumphantly produced the envelope with the money.

"In short," Rene explained, "there has been a continuous party going on at this house all the late afternoon and all evening." Had Bill or Avis called up Lewis's Drugstore at six o'clock, as they usually did, any one of a dozen people would have gladly driven down to the loop and brought them home to share in the festivities.

Michael assured them over and over that he had waited as usual at the drugstore, but nobody called. "Why did you forget to call today?" he wanted to know. It seems he had wasted an hour of the party time sitting on a stool in front of the phone.

"Why, indeed?" Bill mused. "Why today, of all days?"

But David summed the day up best, with his boyish brevity. "I earned three dollars today," he said, "besides the caddy pay that I'll get at the end of the tournament—but Lujean Boyle dropped in and told us she would bring some food from another church social tomorrow, so I guess I'd better give my money to the poor."

Well, what is there to say about things like that? Avis and Bill talked about it from several points of view after the children were finally in bed. Had they done the

things they usually did, it would have been a very pleasant evening for them, too. Had Bill borrowed a nickel
from one of the waitresses and made the usual call to
the children at six o'clock, then the long walk, the fall,
and the "blasphemy" would never have occurred. There
was apparently no excuse for his anxiety and his out-
burst and his remembered suffering at all in this particular experience—or, looking back, in any of the others.
And yet always it had happened the same way. Neither
of them had ever doubted God's watchful care, His
providence, nor had they done things to "build up
credit with Him," so to speak. Theirs was not a
"banker's," but a lover's relationship to God. And yet
the suffering always came to them both—to Avis, usually,
through Bill's rebellion. They had thought long and
often about it in their calmer moments. And tonight
they again did what they had always done when they
tried, after the event, to figure out the mystery of their
particular kind of suffering. They re-examined and medi-
tated together on the life of Christ. They believed that
they were not entirely unaware of the meaning of the
Garden of Gethsemane, of the trial before Pilate, of the
whole history and meaning of the Passion, and they had
always found something particularly significant for themselves in the cry of Christ on the cross: "My God, my
God, why hast Thou forsaken Me?"

"If any one trusted the Father, Christ surely did, and
yet He, too, cried out in agony—" Bill said finally.

After they knelt in prayer, thanking God for the day
Bill turned again to his shelf of Léon Bloy. He wanted
to explore the last few hours with his old friend and
guide (whom he had, of course, never met) and go a
way with this Pilgrim of the Absolute. As he read, he

suddenly remembered a Bloy quotation in one of Raissa
Maritain's books.

"Léon Bloy, with his usual keen perception of the
meaning of suffering, usually explained perfectly the
reason for the acute suffering of people like ourselves,
people who never really doubt the providence of God at
all, and yet invariably (or almost) experience that providence in strange ways," Bill said as he looked through
Raissa Maritain's books. Finding the passage he sought
in *Adventures in Grace* he read aloud to Avis:

When there was no longer any money at all, help would
come from one or another, but always, and as if by fate,
not quickly enough to prevent God from testing the Bloy
family by crucifying days of anxiety.

"That which is altogether peculiar to my case," he wrote
us, "is that the *absolute* certainty of being helped out in
time, in some way or other, never saves me from being
afraid when danger threatens.

"My trust is never shaken, but nothing would be accomplished if God spared me anguish.

"Man would never have been saved if Jesus had not
sweated blood from fear and boredom. *He began to be
dismayed and distressed.* What a text!"

"Always it *is* in time," Avis murmured, "but we just
think it isn't quite, for *in time* means that help will come
before it is actually too late, not just before it is too
late for comfort."

Bill nodded in semi-agreement. "But it is too late in
the usual sense," he said slowly. "Too late to prevent
the refusal of suffering, too late to permit the identification with Christ's suffering. Actually it *is* His mercy
that makes help come too late. He allows us to suffer
with *Him*." He fell silent.

It had been the Walshes' experience, their observation, and they had confirmed it from the writings of those like Bloy who *know*, that *voluntary* suffering is the most active part of the love of God, and that in that kind of suffering men always have to follow Christ *all the way!* "The most mysterious of the many mysterious things He said," Bill resumed after a few moments' silence, "is implied in that cry from the cross: 'My God, my God, why hast Thou forsaken Me?' The *feeling* of being forsaken *even when the mind knows that God never forsakes His creatures* is the paradox upon which is founded the sweet-bitterness of the life of the Christian pilgrimage through this world. And to offer to God the agony of this cry at once from the lips of Christ, and from our own trembling lips, is to offer the whole self . . ."

Avis and Bill had come out of the house again into the late moonlight. They wanted to walk again to the Interurban tracks where Bill had fallen and pray there.

"No, suffering isn't at all like breathing, but it's a lot like breath," Bill said as they walked along. "Or, rather, like the air itself. You take it into yourself in great draughts to sustain life when fatigue and exertion and particularized pain would otherwise strangle your soul. Christ's suffering is *there* all the time (like the air), but it belongs to other people as well as to yourself. You only take your *share*, normally, and you don't much notice it. But in desperation you fill yourself with it, and you know what it is. It is painful for an exhausted man, a suffocating man, to drag air into his lungs, and yet he will do it with his last strength because, like Christ's suffering, it is the deepest necessity of his life.

The suffering of Christ is in the air we breathe. We accept only part of it normally, but we drag it to us in desperation. In real pain we strive for the pure thing, the oxygen of His suffering. When everything else has lost sustaining meaning, we inhale Reality or we die. We have to be empty and gasping to receive it fully. Only so does balance come back to man. Only so does his normal breathing in of life stand revealed to him. Only thus does refreshment and strength come. His capacity has to be enlarged by this forced expansion—"

She walked along, saying little, nodding occasionally, and making little sounds of assent. And then she said, "It is like that around the house, too, with the children. I vow I am going to be patient; that I am not going to raise my voice, but in the end I always do. It is only in some sense when they share what they recognize as my pain and distraction that they are reminded mysteriously of our relationship, just as you are reminded of your relationship to God. There is recognition in suffering, somehow—even children become aware of something vast, mysterious, and true in the presence of blind, outrageous and articulate suffering. It strikes an ancient, buried chord in the human heart, and makes life symphonic somehow."

"My God, my God," he murmured penitently at the place where he had fallen earlier that night. "When hast Thou forsaken me? And *how* hast Thou ever forsaken me? I understand the paradox of *why!*"

They walked along again toward home under the paling stars. Along the horizon of the high plains to the east the rose of dawn was blooming; and the moon was not quite down beyond the western hills. Morning and night were on the horizons, and yet neither day nor night was on the land, but a moment of splendor hovered over earth, a moment in which all things merged and were integrated in beauty so vast that it seemed like high noon of the day of the Resurrection. And in it was the promise of the Ascension and of the "resurrection of the body, and life everlasting."

"It is in their eyes," Bill said to Avis, and she nodded, understanding, as she looked from horizon to horizon across the innocent land. "And it is always somehow in their faces, the unspoiled thing called simplicity by some, and by others childhood. It is neither day nor night with little children, nor dawn nor evening. There is no change of seasons in their look, no history and no foreshadow of events. They look from God at God . . ."

"They seem to look right *through* you, don't they?" Avis mused.

"Yes," Bill answered, "and *Something* looks through their unspoiled, their baptized eyes at all the universe, and laughs deeply and quietly. Francis Thompson knew what he loved when he wrote: 'Look for me in the nurseries of heaven.'"

"I suppose," she said, "that is why all children seem to me like my own, and mine like . . . like His."

"In the young familiar faces," Bill agreed, as they entered their own gate, "is recognition of the design, the pattern—the Providence of God looks out of, and into, their eyes—and in that look is love, tenderness, and the wonderful detachment from this world that is the secret of happiness. There is no fear and no longing in that look, just the fixed gaze and the great understanding serenity. It is a moment of the human story yet outside of it, just as this spacious hour of balanced dawn and moonlight is a moment of time, yet outside both of time and space . . ."

Avis and Bill went into the house which was their home. Their children still slept, though they stirred from time to time—and on each face slept that secret smile, the paradox, as though the children had walked the magic evening-morning and waited now to tell their parents of it, when the sleeping parents should at last awake.

STRIPPED FOR ACTION

༄

PAUL ZENS

THE PROVIDENCE OF GOD can only mean that which is divinely provided to an end. It need not be a miraculous suspension of the laws of nature, nor of the market place. It may only be a readjustment of the laws of chance, as in my case.

One day in the Hürtgen Wald, a German mortar shell burst directly over my head. A piece of shrapnel was blown into the back of my left leg, above the knee. The route of the shrapnel was most remarkable. It passed between the large tendon and the artery, touching neither, and stopped a quarter inch short of the knee joint. A fraction of an inch to the right or left or downward, a larger piece of metal—any one of these near-misses would have been a hit, and I probably would have lost a leg. As it was, all I got was a flesh wound and a permanent incapacity for moving pianos and the like, which I never intended to do anyway.

Had there been no further consequences, I could have gratefully accepted my luck as another, and minor, miracle in the whole series of miraculous escapes and survivals of the war. But incident was co-incident, and coincidence was built into a plot.

I had to spend three months in an Army hospital in a fifty-bed ward. In that place, after a few days, sheer boredom forced the GI's beyond the normal range of their conversation; sometimes even into thought. They all had had at least two years of high school education; they were all as ignorant of ideas as they were knowledgeable about machinery and casual vice. They could read and understand a technical manual; they could not read a book. Some had got as far as western stories; none had heard of the story of the West. Because I had a college degree, I served as a reference book on points of fact. Naturally, they called me "professor," which made me uncomfortable. They meant it kindly enough, but when I graduated I swore a great oath never to enter a school again except to burn it down.

One day (God knows why) this question stirred up an argument: From what country did Columbus sail, and what did he discover? The answer by consensus (I kept quiet) was that Columbus sailed from England and that he discovered the Dutch East Indies.

What a shame! These boys, so competent in fighting and so clever with machinery, were so awkward and so wrong about the simplest intellectual facts. They, who had converted the roads of Europe into so many Main Streets, did not know they had come home. Almost literally, they knew nothing. Their skills at operating and repairing gadgets were worthless when given the kind of problems we have today, and which were apparent even in that winter of 1944. It was not wholly their fault, of course. I decided something should be done; what, exactly, I didn't know. My life had been spared, but for what? If this was Providence, what had been provided?

The answer was not immediately apparent. In the end, it was found, directly and indirectly, by my wife, Susan. We were married in 1940, and in less than a year we learned we were not to have any children. A sudden, serious, and painful operation—painful physically and emotionally—was necessary. When the shock began to wear off, we talked about adopting children, as our friends urged. But the times were bad: Susan's health was poor for a long time, and before she had recovered I was drafted.

During the war we exchanged letters that were vaguely hopeful about the future. After the war we began the translation of the hopes into action by taking stock. We found a curious inventory. There were all assets and no liabilities. We were absolutely free to go anywhere, and to do anything we chose. We had no property to manage, no children to care for. We had severance pay and no debts. The Hand of Providence, if it was Providence, had stripped us of all impedimenta of normal responsibility. We were rather like Adam and Eve in the beginning.

We took to the woods. Both of us were city-born and city-bred, and both of us, during the war, discovered we were not city people after all. Susan confessed to a long-suppressed love for birds and flowers and trees. I had learned that the earth, which supports life, is the best protection for life. We agreed that the proper culture is first of all agriculture. In the process of making an industrial and commercial culture, the meaning of the word "dirt" had been altered and debased. Cities, which cover up the dirt, are dirty; the country, where the dirt is exposed, is clean. So the war, then, gave us that opportunity for the clean break which everybody hopes for.

It seemed perfectly simple and rational to us. When our friends pointed out that we probably would not make much money, we agreed we probably wouldn't; money was relevant, but secondary. Still, we had not decided on what was primary.

Farming was an obvious possibility; and impossible. The work was too heavy for either of us. I tried writing newspaper editorials; but I thought the U.S. should support Europe, and the editor did not; so we parted. And, anyway, ex-GI's do not read editorials.

After a year and a half of such fooling around, Susan took command. The answer to what we should do was obvious to everybody, except me. Susan had been hinting, making suggestions, asking questions. Now she gave orders. (I often wonder whether the Providence of God is a Determined Woman.)

"You," she said, "are going to be a teacher. That's what you're fit for, and all you're fit for. You go right up to Pittsfield and see Scott Buchanan."

Naturally, I went.

There was a plan at the time to start a new college in the Berkshires, and Scott Buchanan was to be the Dean. He was most courteous and sympathetic. I had only an A.B. degree, but since the college would not open for a year or two I had time to get an M.A., the "union card." As it turned out, the college never did open; but his kindness and encouragement, added to Susan's convictions, were what I needed in order to mind my real business.

Once the resolve was made—in the face of the "normal American" distaste for schooling—the series of coincidences piled up in a most convincing way. I could not go to graduate school unless I had more income than the

L

G.I. bill provided. We had bought a house and the mortgage bills had to be paid. But it was July (1947), the poorest possible time to find the combination we needed: a graduate school which would accept my application for entrance and also give me a job. But within a month we had both at the University of New Hampshire, a bull's-eye on the first shot.

There I worked under a former Protestant minister (American sociology, my subject, was founded by ex-ministers) who admitted that if he ever did join a church, it would be the Catholic Church. At the end of the first semester a teaching job in the School of Agriculture became unexpectedly available, and I got that. That my first course, my very own, should be teaching Rural Sociology in an agricultural school, was, at least, the most solid of confirmatory omens. Susan was restrained in her comments, but she looked like a well-fed cat. We also sold our house at a profit.

From New Hampshire I went to Yale to get my doctorate. It is always advisable to teach while working for a Ph. D., and the first position I applied for, I got.

Now observe again the firm clutch of Providence. While I had always more or less disliked schools, I never much objected to learning; at least I had always bought books. I have a taste for oblique approaches to American history; and I used to think how much fun a history course would be if we could forget treaties, dates and generals, and get at the real news in history. Well, the first course I was asked to teach was American History. So we began with cowboys and Indians fighting about land; and everybody had a lot of fun.

So here we are in an isolated place in the Vermont hills. I am now teaching Sociology as an unabashed

Catholic in a non-sectarian college. Since all college students are radicals, as everyone knows, we present orthodoxy as the radix; since the modern family and the modern economy have gone to pot, we are trying to save both by putting the family back in the *oikos;* since religion is a grim reality, we see it as a picturesque romance. All of these things we do formally in class, and informally at home, where the students come in groups or individually to be enlightened, or soothed or amused. The only indication of religious venom shown so far is the epithet "egg-nog sticks" applied (by a Unitarian, of all people) to the Agnostics. Along with the art teacher (who admits the Catholic religion is the only possible religion if you have to have one, because it has produced great art), we work for the greater glory of God.

This story seems to violate all the rules. Providence has not intervened with last-minute rescues—we were never in peril; there were no obstacles in the always smooth road. We faced no severe tests of virtue or endurance. It is not so much a matter of what we were given as of what we were left. We were stripped for action. Quite clearly, the story is not finished. We have no idea of what will happen next (professors are gifted with hindsight, not prophecy). After five years we have learned that the next move is always plainly indicated, and I no longer have to be beaten about the head to be alerted. Sufficient unto the day is the Providence thereof.

A RED BRICK SCHOOLHOUSE

GRACE ELIZABETH ROGAN

JOHN HERSHEY'S shocking report on Hiroshima affected many people very deeply, but for us it is wholly unforgettable, since indirectly it changed the course of our lives.

In 1946 we celebrated our first wedding anniversary. We had one child, a son David, aged one month, and we were living in a garage apartment on an estate in northern Illinois. Temporarily, we thought, for, as is the case with many young families, our eyes were turned longingly toward the land. We wanted to raise our children where there was light, space and air for all, and where we could daily see examples of God's creativeness about us. We wanted to work for ourselves and the sons and daughters to come, a joy instead of a drudgery. We wanted, in fact, a whole and holy life.

Now, as a matter of fact, we were already living in the country, but we were not yet on the land. For although we were surrounded by beautiful views of wood and lake, wide stretches of carefully tended lawns, and row upon row of cultivated flowers, there was no soil of our own here in which we could put down our roots. So we dreamed constantly of a place of our own with enough space for a garden, chickens and a cow—in other words, a homestead. But our dream shrank in the broad light of day. We were poor, my husband acquiring his first teaching experience in a country school; our friends were poor too, and if there were any generous-hearted philanthropist about who delighted in helping young families like ourselves, we did not know him.

In December that year we went to Loveland, Ohio to spend the Christmas holiday at Grailville, School of the Apostolate for young women. A year in the country on our own had been a good test of our spiritual and mental resources, but it had made us feel the need for a time of renewal and inspiration. And the days spent in taking the fullest possible part in the Christmas liturgy—praying, rejoicing and playing with others in the spirit of Christ—were refreshing. It was an added and unexpected pleasure when we met two young couples who were living in the neighborhood. They were eager to establish homes with a sound Christian family life and hoped that eventually they would have more neighbors with the same ideals. One delightful evening spent with them ended with a suggestion: "Would you be interested in coming here to live?"

Our response was enthusiastic but not too definite. We talked and thought about the possibility on the train trip home. But the move did not seem a very likely solution to our problems. It would involve buying property including a house, or purchasing land and building ourselves, and we had not a penny over our weekly needs. It also meant a change of job for the breadwinner of the family. We put the idea away for the time being and turned our minds instead towards the possibility of join-

ing friends who had recently moved to Minnesota. There
were openings in the teaching field there, and perhaps
we could rent a house in the country for a few years
before we began to think of buying land.

But God had His own plans for us and He began to
write straight with crooked lines. Soon after our return
home a letter from one of our Grailville friends arrived:
"There's a place up for sale that seems just right for you,"
it read. "A house, three acres, chicken house, reasonably
priced and good neighbors. Can you come down and
look at it?" Well, the sum needed was an unheard-of
amount for us. Since this opportunity had come out of
the blue, however, with no effort on our part, it did not
seem our doing but the Lord's, and we felt we should
show Him some co-operation. Jim had a one-room
schoolhouse full of children to teach, so he was unable
to make the trip. We had no loving grandmothers close
by, so I bundled David up and left him with our good
friends at Blessed Martin House in Chicago, thus beginning his interracial interests early in life. After that, there
I was, on my way house-hunting.

Shortly after my arrival in Loveland, a friend took me
to see the property. As we tramped across the fields, a
stiff March wind in our faces, I rejoiced in everything—
the brilliant flash of a cardinal against the gray-brown
boughs, the raw look of the newly plowed fields. Fr. Hopkins' words were singing in my head,

Nothing is so beautiful as spring—
    When weeds, in wheels, shoot long and lovely and lush;
    Thrush's eggs look little low heavens, and thrush
Through the echoing timber does so rinse and wring
The ear, it strikes like lightnings to hear him sing;
    The glassy peartree leaves and blooms, they brush

 The descending blue; that blue is all in a rush
With richness; the racing lambs too have fair their fling.°

But disappointment awaited us. The house was not all
we had hoped for, and the price was too high for the
value of the land. Later on, back in the warm and comfortable kitchen of the home where I was staying, a conference resulted in the decision that I should remain at
least a week and look around the countryside for other
possibilities.

 It was a busy week. We started out early each morning
and looked at houses of all shapes and sizes. But we could
not find the one that was our shape and size, especially
one to fit our imaginary bank account. Towards the end
of my week's stay I was beginning to feel desperate. It
seemed as though we had mistaken a whim of our own
for a hint from God. At a second conference with the
family I was staying with, we decided to call upon the
saints and see if they could give us some light on the
situation. I stayed for another week—a full and merry
one, during which several friendly families (of varied
racial extraction) besieged their favorite saints with
pleas to "find the Rogans a home." What a week that
must have been in Heaven! It was the month of March,
and Saints Patrick, Joseph and Benedict were all on trial.
What Irishman among us was not sure, begorra, that
Saint Patrick would do the job? But we went out with a
real estate agent that day, and still nothing promising
showed itself. Our Irish stronghold of prayer held out
that night until eleven o'clock, but then gave up with a
muttered apology about all the people who would be
beseeching Saint Patrick for something on his feastday.

° "Spring," from *Poems*, by Gerard Manley Hopkins (Oxford).

Since we were two generations removed from the ould sod, we would just have to wait our turn.

Another family who outdid themselves in generosity, giving time and energy to my search for a house, were certain that Saint Joseph could not fail. Did not the man of the family have an ace up his sleeve, since his middle name was Joseph, and how could a patron saint deny his own? For reasons we shall never know until we meet him in Heaven, Saint Joseph did not come through that day. Now we had one hope left. And may I say, though I was not too specific about it that day, I knew all along that Saint Benedict would manage? Jim and I were Oblates of his order, and who knew better than our Father Benedict the physical setting we needed to put into practice his tradition of *Ora et labora?*

So you will not be surprised to hear that on the Feast of Saint Benedict, 1946, we found our home. The real estate agent, who had taken us on several fruitless trips, apologized as he drove us down the road. He knew by this time that we were in the "lower-class bracket," and he did not have too much to offer us. "After all, if you can't go beyond six-ten. . . ." he would say. So he had no hope that this last place he was going to show us would suit us any better than the previous ones. We slowed down and he pointed, rather hesitantly, to a red brick building.

"Oh," I groaned, "Jim will have nightmares if he has to live in a one-room schoolhouse as well as teach in one." With this cheerful introduction, we began our inspection. But as we went from room to room, our family life began to take shape before my eyes. There was a spacious, sunlit kitchen, just the place for family .easts and celebrations. Another room was just right for the children, and here was space enough to have small friends in to play on rainy days. Upstairs was all one huge room, floored and plastered but still unfinished, low-ceilinged, many-windowed, inviting. In my mind's eye I could see it full, people square-dancing, sitting on cushions on the floor, enjoying a picnic supper, singing and laughing. (A few months later the picture came true, through the miracle of a building becoming a home.)

Our property—I was already calling it "ours"—included a chicken house, a garage and a huge barn made of sturdy, seasoned oak, plus eleven acres of flat, tillable land. My decision was immediate. I had to catch a five o'clock train in the afternoon, and by that time I had succeeded in borrowing $190 to add to the $10 I had, making the necessary $200 payment to hold the house. My husband always starts the family legend by saying, "My wife bought our home for $10." He still chuckles when he recalls the day he answered a long-distance call to discover that his wife had the deed to a red brick schoolhouse and eleven acres in her pocket. In such a simple and uncomplicated way did he become a land-owner.

But in order to own land one must buy it. We had known this all along but had not yet faced the problem of raising the money even for the down payment. We had to raise $2,000 in sixty days, and we might just as well have been told $10,000. We did not know where to begin. But do not think we were discouraged. I was already choosing colors for the rooms and materials for curtains. We had married trusting in God's providence, and He had taken care of our needs time and again.

As the days hurried by, however, and no money appeared, I must confess that I began to have my private doubts. I am afraid I really thought we were asking too much of God this time. But my husband is a man of great faith. If God wants us to live in this growing community of Catholic families, if this is the house He has in mind for us, then the money will come, he assured me. And if it did not? Then it would be evident that these plans were our own, and God had something else in mind for us. How should we raise the money? Neither of our families at the time were able to help, and our friends were as poor as ourselves. We should sow the money, my husband explained. We should take what money we could scrape together and send it to someone who was in desperate need. Our Lord would reward our sowing an hundredfold.

Now to return to the bearing of John Hershey's report on our lives, which you have patiently waited to have explained. Just at this time someone gave us a copy. We read it, and were appalled by the terrible sufferings which the people there had endured and at the devastation of the city. We knew at once where we should sow our widow's mite. There were poor in our own country we well knew, through our close contacts with the *Catholic Worker*, Friendship House and Blessed Martin Center. But this was an immediate need and a desperate one. So we took ten dollars from our small weekly budget and, since we wanted this to be a true giving, a real sacrifice, we took it from the food money for the week. We sent the sum to the address of a priest in Hiroshima which was listed in the pages of the *Catholic Worker*. And on that day we began a novena to Saint Joseph, foster-father of Our Lord, patron of families. Surely he who always found a home for the Holy Family would listen to our plea.

And now begins the account of our personal miracle. Less than a week later we received a special delivery letter, with an enclosure, from our friends at Grailville, telling us that we had qualified for a homestead loan in the amount of $1,000. We had not even known that they were inquiring about this for us! We were stunned. We had never handled that sum of money before and were not likely to again. But when we had recovered from our astonishment we came back to reality and realized that we still had only half of what we needed. So we turned with renewed fervor to Saint Joseph, and included prayers to our Father Benedict, who had found that truly Benedictine home for us—a house large enough to become a place of hospitality.

On the Feast of the Solemnity of Saint Joseph, the concluding day of our novena, we received a telephone call from Loveland. They had been trying to reach us for several days, but a nationwide telephone strike had made it impossible.

How much money had we raised? they asked. Jim answered quickly. We had received a check for $1,000 but had not been able to do anything about the other $1,000, and since our sixty-day deadline was almost due, it looked as though we might have to forego our "schoolhouse." "Don't worry," they said, "we have the other $1,000 here for you. Come down on the next train if you can possibly manage it!"

Again David was bundled off to Blessed Martin Center. And again I headed for Ohio. My only memory of that train ride is the one big question that kept revolving in my racing thoughts: Where *did* the money come from? And here is the second installment of our particular miracle. One of the young married men who had greatly encouraged the idea of our moving had been invited to

a dinner given by a Catholic group in the city. He had
mentioned to a friend, who sat next to him, the plight
of a family he knew who were hoping to move to the
country but couldn't raise the money to buy the house
and land they wanted.

"How much do they need?" the friend asked. "A
thousand dollars." Pause. "I think I can help them out,"
said the young man at last. He had never seen or even
heard of us until that evening! He and his wife had that
amount in the bank. They were saving for a house of
their own, but at the present time were renting a place
in the country near his work. They had not decided
where they would settle permanently, so they did not, at
the moment, need the money. And they would be happy
to help another young family who shared with them the
same ideals of Christian family life.

The loan was made, in due course, with no interest and
no set time of payment. The only provision was that we
would do the same thing for another family if we ever
had the chance.

If we had needed proof that God answers prayers, and
often in a most direct manner, we certainly had it now.
We saw too that it is the poor who help the poor. The
young couple who came to our rescue had very little in
the way of material possessions, aside from this sum in
the bank, and still they would not keep the money for
security in face of someone else's more pressing need.

God's provident care for a family (as well as all individuals) is loving, constant, never-ending. We have
experienced this from the beginning of our married life
and in a particular manner when we were attempting to
settle permanently as a family. Our move was only the
beginning of many changes. My husband had been

teaching in a rural school. We had neither time nor opportunity to investigate the job situation in our new location before we moved, but we found summer work and soon afterwards, a teaching position, starting in the fall.

The four-hundred-mile trip to our new home was made in a 1937 Chevrolet, a careworn model with no spare tire, and it was accomplished without the slightest mishap, but when we arrived at our destination, the car stopped and did not go again until its burnt-out battery was replaced.

Friends showered us with love and material aid during those first weeks of settling in our new home. The first sight that greeted our eyes was a plowed field, only waiting to be seeded. A community project made light work of planting a good-sized garden, and an old-style painting bee rapidly transformed the battle-ship gray walls to warm, bright colors. But the final gift that made of a property a homestead was a brooder full of baby chicks.

We join daily with King David when he sings, "With justice, by wondrous signs, thou hearest us, O God our Saviour." We pray that our story of God's goodness and love will inspire other families. Our Lord has told us that if we seek first the kingdom of God and His Justice, everything else will be given to us. We know this to be true.

Our world today is crying out for saints. And saints will come from devout Christian homes where husband and wife are living in the love of Christ. There are factors in modern society which make life for a newly married couple without financial means seem full of the most terrifying difficulties. The housing shortage continues, large families are discouraged and ridiculed, and war clouds darken the skies. But if we use our spiritual weapons of faith, prayer and trust in God's providence, many of these difficulties will be overcome.

God is eager for us to establish Christian homes. The kind of home Father Vann describes:

The family that is living in love will be one of those homes where the doors seem always to be open and the rooms always full—full of all sorts of oddities as well as all sorts of loveliness, full of the waifs and strays of society as well as the immediate circle of friends, full because you find there at all times the unassuming glory of charity, which is love and reverence for every human being and the warmth and welcome of home.

May the young Catholic families of our times willingly co-operate with God in this work of grace.

SIX AREN'T ENOUGH

∽

BILL MORGAN

WE FIRST BEGAN to realize that we might some day have a big family when we found that John, our second boy, was góing to follow fast on the heels of Jim, the oldest. We had been married less than a year and a half. We had a nice little home, rent very low, some distance out of town, and my job seemed pretty secure. In fact, we were already working overtime in the shop with defense work. As I look back now, things really looked pretty hopeful. Jim, who had been too frail to take home from the hospital for several weeks, had long since made up for lost time. I don't remember now how he looked, but Ellen insisted he was the most beautiful baby she had ever seen. But she's said that about each of them in turn since then.

Somewhere we had both remembered hearing that a child is truly a gift from God. And it seemed like such a beautiful way of expressing the joy of seeing ourselves repeated in our firstborn. We blissfully used that expression in talking of babies with other married couples. The indulgent smile we got left us cold, and it wasn't long before we realized that babies were not considered gifts

159

of God at all. I don't think that either of us ever mentioned that idea again until a few months ago.

And then with the same simpleness that had led us to believe that babies were gifts from God, we let our friends in on the good news about the second baby's coming. We found out right away that we had done something not quite right.

"Wow—that'll be two kids in less than fourteen months!"

"What are you trying to do, Morgan, set a record?"

"How's Ellen taking it? I hope she's feeling all right."

"Well, that's going to be real nice, having your family right at the start so you can grow up with them . . . I wish we had done that with our two."

In general, though, our friends were quite sympathetic and life seemed pretty good. Jim was practically no care at all. The joys of making a home and caring for a baby of her own and trying new recipes kept Ellen contented. We used to read letters and articles in women's magazines and in the newspapers telling how a new baby had driven a wedge between some man and his wife—she loved the baby and forgot about her husband, or the father resented the baby taking so much of his wife's time, or the wife feared another childbirth so much that she lived in constant fear—well, we'd read the stuff and look at each other and wonder what they were talking about.

John came into the world late in the fall. Ten days later we were all home together, the bills were paid, the house was comfortable, our boys were both well and strong, and we were all happy.

On her check-up visit the doctor was pretty definite in advising Ellen not to have another baby for a while

She asked him to be honest and tell her just where she
might expect trouble. He couldn't give her any definite
answer. (We found out later that this is routine advice
today for most doctors to give.) But he did remind her
she'd had two babies in just over a year, and even if she
were in good health—well, it just wasn't the thing to do.
So at least we had been warned.

Our conversation with other young Catholic couples
switched from talking about babies to talking about not
having babies. No one, it seemed, thought one could
depend on Rhythm, but what can one do about it? We
started reading the church-rack pamphlets on birth control, and read the familiar book by the Latz Foundation.
I guess that by the time we found out that God planned
Dan to follow John by fourteen months, we were fully
in accord with the righteousness of "planning a family
the way *we* wanted and could care for them."

In the meantime we'd had an opportunity to buy a
home "on a shoestring." After moving, there were hundreds of jobs that just had to be done at once. The new
house did look pretty shabby, and after we found Dan
was coming we made up our minds to show our friends
that having a family didn't mean we couldn't have a
home of our own, too. So we worked and worked. We
wallpapered and painted. Ellen would hold boards and
help measure while I sawed. We even dug a new wall,
with no help. We worked every night and every week-
end for months and months.

But it began to tell on Ellen. All this work and no sign
of a let-up—and another baby coming in early winter.
That we surely hadn't counted on when we bought the
house. There were only two bedrooms—what if it were
a girl? And why did God want to make it so hard for us?

M

Neither of us had ever been a particularly strong Catholic. Ellen's folks, who weren't wealthy at all, had made the mistake of sending her to a wealthy girls' Catholic high school. Along with algebra, French and dramatics, she learned that one's success in married life was (and still is, I guess) judged by the speed and manner in which one acquired an apartment, good-looking clothes, a car, furniture, an annual vacation trip, one baby, two children, in that order.

Now the pressure would really be on. We knew better than to tell anyone we were going to have another baby, until it couldn't be kept a secret any longer. We knew enough never to bring the subject right out for discussion. One hints about it in a roundabout, gay manner, as if it's sort of a joke on one, finding one is going to have another baby. Ellen's folks didn't say anything; they had had a big family themselves. They felt sorry for us, but the rest of her family were not so charitable: "She ought to know better than to ruin her health." "You can't ever be normal or happy with kids coming one after another like that." One hears that from enough people, many of them apparently meaning well, and one gets to believing it after a while. Furthermore, we didn't really know of anyone who had ever had children so close together.

Dan came into the world big and healthy, quite oblivious to his parents' complexes, and was baptized right after the New Year. Now we had another chance! After all, three children were not too many, even though we had been married but three years. The house kept our minds off our worries. Each week-end's work always was planned far ahead of time. When Saturday overtime became standard, progress nearly stopped on the house, but to compensate for it we found we were earning more money than we'd ever dreamed possible.

By the time Dan was almost a year old, there was still no sign of a baby on the way. We had been able to save a few hundred dollars in bonds. Maybe God wasn't so unjust to us after all. Maybe we wouldn't end up with a whole houseful of kids. By careful planning and saving we'd be able to send the three boys to a good Catholic high school and college. And they wouldn't have to feel different from the crowd.

For the first time in our married life we found ourselves thinking like the "don't havers." Once one starts raising a big family one starts classifying Catholics into one of two kinds: those that have a big family and those that don't. The ninety per cent or so that don't may never have been able to. They may want more children badly, or they may be, like so many are, "spacing" children with the spaces awfully far apart after the third baby. But whatever their reasons, when one feels that God is burdening one with children others should have had (and that's the way we sometimes felt, I'm ashamed to say) one puts all the "don't havers" on one side of the line and oneself and a few others on the other side.

Since then we've thought about this many times and talked it over with others who have tried raising a big family on a Sunday-morning ration of Catholicism. And except for those who get strong moral support from their families or friends, nearly all of them felt this same temptation to judge others, often very unfairly.

Well, we had, for no apparent reason, and with some misgivings, joined the ranks of the "don't havers." We began having money to spend on just "extras." We knew the house we were in never would do, so we began to look for a better home. We hunted and hunted, and called, I believe, every real estate office in town. But this was a boom town and the price of the kind of home we wanted was already out of our reach. We finally gave up hunting.

Then it was that we discovered another baby was on the way. This time Ellen was just tired out and blue almost constantly. The children were good; we'd always kept firm discipline, but three boys are still three boys. We were in the same boat all over again, only this time it was just that much worse. Ellen felt so bad about the way things were going that she stopped going to Confession for many months. She knew it was wrong to feel the way she did, but there was no use trying to feel sorry for it. I used to get peeved at her because she didn't even want to try pulling out of it. I remember pulling all the tricks, buying her something pretty and praising her, or taking over care of the boys when I came home from work. I guess I tried everything but understanding her. Both of us had had Catholic homes and schooling, thank God, and the memory of them kept us going through the routine of church on Sunday. But I had to keep my mind a blank when these thoughts would start closing in on me: "Why does God pick on *us?* Why couldn't He give us just a little more time? Doesn't He know that the mess we're in will prove to the 'don't havers' that they're right?"

We were back in the ranks of the "havers" for sure, but now we were in a class by ourselves. Four kids in less than five years! We drew apart from everyone as much as we could. We knew the advice, sarcastic and solicitous, would soon be coming, so we tried to avoid exposing ourselves to it as much as possible. A man can laugh or shrug off this kind of hypocrisy, but it isn't so easy for a mother. What hurt Ellen most of all were the seemingly endless uncharitable remarks of other women, especially Catholics who ought to know better. Thank God we had a few close friends who were either neutral or who felt as we did about raising a Christian family.

And then, a few months before Mary was to arrive, we found a house, better than we had ever hoped for, right on the edge of town. It had enough bedrooms, a big back yard and a garden. It was old, and it cost more than we could really afford, but it was wonderful. We sold our other home as it was and moved in here as soon as we could. We are in this home, we hope, for the rest of our lives.

The job of moving and cleaning and painting helped keep our minds off our troubles. When the time came in the fall, Ellen's aunt took care of the boys while she was in the hospital with Mary. Believe it or not, the Morgans really had a baby girl of their own. I'll never forget the dreamy look in Ellen's eyes when I tiptoed into her room a few minutes after Mary was born. "She's a girl, Bill, a girl! Just think—our own little girl!" And she closed her eyes for that long, wonderful sleep of a new mother.

Just the thought of a little girl put new life in both of us. After all, four children weren't so bad—we had a home big enough to hold all of them and more. I was working long hours on secret war work, so money was plentiful. Best of all, Ellen was feeling wonderful again. Mary and the boys were all as healthy as could be.

We often look back and talk over the change that took place in our lives with Mary's coming. Somehow or other, the arrival of Betty less than a year and a half later seemed perfectly natural. Ellen was up to her ears in work, the mending pile grew larger instead of smaller, but the important things got done. We still can't understand it, but it seemed the larger the family got, the calmer and less irritable we got. Things that bothered us before seemed unimportant to us now. Our home wasn't any less attractive; things were just better-organized. Ellen and I both became more efficient and, what's more, we liked it. The older children were starting to be of some help with chores around the house, and disciplining five turned out to be no worse than training three. The youngsters amused and taught each other.

By the time Betty came, our circle of friends had changed almost completely. Ellen's high school friends had dropped away (or she had dropped them) one by one. Several out of her class of over a hundred were married and having families, and when we heard of them we looked them up, making some wonderful new friends. Now and then some one would say a few sincere words of encouragement to us, particularly older parents whose children were grown. That helped a lot. Younger girls started coming occasionally to Ellen for advice, and instead of my family being the butt of jokes at work, it became more of a curiosity. Some of the men had a genuine interest, so I kept them amused (and still do) with the never-ending comedy of watching the Morgan kids grow up.

We began to read Catholic literature in earnest, and found the answers to most of the "don't havers'" assumptions. We started to ask embarrassing questions, instead of being "nice" and just listening. Ellen realized suddenly that if one really believes in what one is saying and offers a little prayer to the Holy Ghost while talking, one usually says the right thing. One can break down that false front of righteousness that most of the "baby spacers" assume and leave them flat, or at a point where

further discussion is ridiculous. One can smile while
doing it, and they'll leave still one's friends.

Ann, our youngest, is now almost a year old. Next year
the boys will all be in school. (The thrill of having our
oldest make his First Holy Communion is overwhelming.) With each of the six children, aside from the great
spiritual uplift which was sometimes hidden, has come a
material boost in the form of a raise or promotion, or
some other obvious gift which could be nothing else but
God's providence. But with Ann came the greatest gift
of all—the realization of what being a Catholic, and particularly a Catholic parent, really means.

Integrity has helped us to part of that great realization.
Many other good books and magazines have helped, too.
We believe one of the greatest helps was the opportunity
to attend a Family Renewal Day; in some places they
are called Cana Conferences. We spent a full Sunday
listening to lectures on the problems of marriage today.
There were frank question-and-answer periods that got
right down to earth. Father told us what marriage means
as a Sacrament, how every good act in marriage develops
man and wife, bringing them closer to God. We learned,
for the first time, that in creating life, man and wife are
fulfilling the highest goal of the Sacrament of Matrimony, and that the creation of life requires a separate
and distinct action on the part of Almighty God. Co-
operating with man and wife, He infuses into the tiny
cell at the moment of conception an immortal soul.

We learned that we're having such an awful time trying to figure out "the connection between religion and
life" simply because the whole world we live in has, in
the last thirty years or so, turned almost completely to
paganism, with here and there a humanitarian, Protes-

tant veneer. Today we are all being trained in the school of selfishness, from the day we are born. We go to Catholic schools, listen to Catholic sermons and belong to Catholic organizations, but we "don't get the connection." Our whole lives are so emasculated with materialistic ideals that many a Catholic is proud that he can be a Catholic and not have to be *different*—like the "Christian Scientists, who can't even call a doctor" or "the Jehovah Witnesses, who always look so unhappy selling anti-religious magazines on the streets."

That same kind of thinking makes it very easy for parents to justify not having a baby until after they are married a few years (when two people are "well adjusted" to each other), not realizing that sharing the job and the joy of caring for their own flesh and blood will bring them closer together than reading a whole library of books on marriage. Selfishness must lie behind many of the arguments of Catholic parents who talk about wanting "quality in their children instead of quantity." But any nun or C.Y.O. chaplain, or policeman or court judge, will tell one that, other things being equal, children from a big family are just as intelligent, better disciplined, better adjusted, more wholesome, more unselfish, and more trusting than children from a family of one or two.

I often wonder, as I look up and down the tables at the monthly Holy Name Communion Breakfast, how many of the men realize that by refusing to rear a big family they are endangering their souls and the souls of their children. We have no exact statistics to compare relative family size in our own parish, a typically young and active parish, with an equal number of pagan or Protestant families, but we have made it a point in the last several months to note family sizes and attitudes toward family size in talking to Catholics and non-Catholics alike, and there doesn't seem to be much effective difference. Although the number of so-called Catholics who use contraceptives must be terrible, the birth prevention slogans have been pretty well accepted as truths by almost all Catholics. What else can account for the very few families of more than four in the average city parish today? We can't judge individuals, but it's folly to say we mustn't judge whole parishes.

In all the years we've been married, other than at our Family Renewal Day, neither of us has heard one word from the pulpit on the glory and the joy and the grace that God reserves for the parents and the children in a big family living His way. We've heard scarcely anything on the real purpose of marriage. We're all proud of our schools and our churches, but how many of us are as worried about the souls of the children that must some day be supplied to fill them? Because of today's prosperity, many couples are having children because they can afford them and still have a pleasant life. But what about the next slump? If children are last on the list, what good will our empty schools be then?

If the creation of life is the highest goal of marriage, it seems that we ought to hear occasional sermons reminding all of us about just that. If God planned the Christian family for two thousand years, we ought to be able to trust Him more than our pagan doctors. If the divorce and domestic trouble rate goes up directly as the number of children in a family goes down, we ought to see the handwriting on the wall.

Looking back on our own experience, it's easy to see how the burdens we resented were the means by which

God was to give us the grace really to begin living for the first time in our lives. Most young Catholic couples start out without too much prejudice against a normal family. They're willing to be "freaks" in the eyes of the world and heroes in the eyes of God, if they can just get a little moral support from their friends, from other Catholics, and from their pastors.

The social and economic pressure against a real family puts normal parents on the defensive, so much so that they now exert little influence in life almost anywhere. Normal families ought instead to be getting together. Think of what a tremendous influence such families, aware of their kinship in the Mystical Body of Christ, and strengthened by their trust in the Holy Ghost and in each other, could have on the whole environment. A big family has always been one of God's greatest gifts. Today it has a special meaning because it can't but change the direction of one's whole life and the lives of one's children and their children, long after all of us are gone.

MARRIAGE AND SPIRITUALITY

ᏨᏜᏗ

MARY REED NEWLAND

I HAVE A FRIEND who is a career-girl, single and very attractive. Marriage, she says, is not her dish of tea. All of which annoys most of her female friends, and they are forever trying to expose her to the right kind of man and what they call her kind of marriage, ever hopeful that some day it will take. "Jane," they say, "you just don't understand how wonderful marriage can be. You haven't seen the right kind of marriages—or you wouldn't be so hard to convince."

So it was no surprise to have them descend one day with the announcement that "this is it"—they had the perfect couple lined up, and all she had to do was meet them and she'd be converted. She met them and marvelled at how they were, indeed, perfect in every way— charming, devoted, beautifully adjusted, living in the perfect apartment, he the perfect provider and she the perfect homemaker and companion. It was too good to be true, and for the first time she was ready to concede that marriage didn't necessarily have to be more bickering than bliss.

Then, several months later, the man phoned with the

shattering announcement that things were about to crack up. Would she come and talk to the light of his life? He had taken a severe beating in the market, their finances had done a right-about-face, and suddenly life was real, life was earnest. He was able to bear up under it, but apparently she wasn't, and what with having to give up a few pleasures and buckle down to a job, she was about ready to fly the coop. Jane was a working girl and happy in her job; maybe it would help if she'd give her a career-girl type of pep talk. So Jane hiked over one night to listen to the whole tale of woe. This is how it went:

"My dear, you can't know what a mess it all is. I hate working, but I have to or we can't live the way we do, and Jack simply doesn't understand what it's doing to me. Then to complicate things even more, his mother's been here for two weeks, and I had to move all my clothes out and take a temporary apartment downstairs."

"Why the apartment downstairs? Don't tell me you can't put up with your mother-in-law for just two weeks?"

"My mother-in-law?"—and the other woman screamed —"Oh darling! You don't understand—we aren't even married!"

Marriage is a *spiritual union*. People can do all the things that are permitted in marriage outside of marriage —and there is no union. The whole thing hangs together because God says it does, and He feeds it a special kind of grace, grace reserved for the married alone; then He tells them what they are to be to one another, and He says that doing these things, they will give honor and glory to Him, for which reason He created them in the first place. He says the whole thing, from falling in love and making the decision to marry, to exchanging vows and giving each other freely in physical union, and to the ultimate end of the physical union, the bearing of children—all this, He says, is a holy vocation, a *calling* through which He calls us to Himself. This is how the married serve God—and it differs from any other vocation because it depends upon your loving and serving first of all one specific person, a husband or a wife, and secondly these specific children—and the love that is perfected in the service of these is the love we will know for all men.

But it's not easy, being married. It looks easy because we find our way to it through a series of shattering experiences with physical attraction (I do not mean sin—but just the discovery that we are capable of wanting to possess someone, and be possessed, in the full physical sense of the word); and because we know it first in the terms of physical love, we are apt to measure love forever after in these same terms. It isn't that at all. Physical love imitates God's love for the soul; when it is pure, it is good. After all, God invented it, and all through Scripture His love for His Church is described in what some souls consider the most shocking physical language. All you have to do is read the Canticle of Canticles to come away with the conviction that God knows all about physical love and with the conviction that it's a pretty exalted thing. It's an exalted thing—call it a facet of an exalted thing—but it is not the whole, nor will it last forever. Even in marriages that are unmarred by more than just ordinary every-day trials, it peters out, the passion is spent and the fires banked and it becomes obvious that it has been only a means and not an end. It is a kind of *hors d'oeuvre*—a hint of things to come. It hints of a love that is waiting to be found but which, for lack of other words, must be described in the terms of physical desire.

We ought to know all this when we realize that physical love is easy—you literally "fall" into it. Those whose vocation is marriage do not have to sit down and talk themselves into falling in love. It happens without any very apparent reason. And even for those who have not had the benefit of clinical texts on how to go about the specific act of nuptial lovemaking, instinct tells them what it is all about. Along with this, there goes with that first impassioned desire to possess and be possessed an equally impassioned desire to serve. Nothing is too much for the beloved, nothing too good. Nothing can be asked of us that we would not already want to give. All happiness is bound up in the happiness of the beloved, and there is none outside of him. He is perfect—if not quite perfect, at least unique—and no one else is the combination of humor and wisdom and kindness and beauty that he is. Foolish? Of course it is foolish, in a way. No one is as perfect as that. But that is how love makes people look perfect, and it's a very good thing, because one ought not go about getting married to merely a physique. These are the spiritual qualities we see, and this is the first step toward spiritual love. This is why it is all wrong to pooh-pooh physical love—it is an uncanny imitation of spiritual love, and for some people (those called to marriage), it is the way to spiritual love.

So—we get married, and life is going to be beer and skittles ever after. Of course, there's that little matter of "for better, for worse, for richer, for poorer, in sickness and in health," but who cares? To people who love each other as we do, nothing can make any difference. We are two minds with but a single thought—that we love each other. Whatever differences there are between us are the happy physical differences—they merely complement each other. Our marriage is going to be different from any other, we are going to be the exception. We both understand that we are called to be saints—we will be saints together. We have found a framework designed by God in which we can give ourselves to each other and still give ourselves to God. How easy!

What a sweet delirium—and God is kind to permit it. Because without the sweetness and the convictions, we would never have the courage to start. It is like the first abandon of a soul completely converted to a desire for nothing but God's will. I remember talking to a friend once and telling her that was how we had to love God's will—with abandon. And she said, hesitantly, "Yes—but I'm afraid. Afraid that if I do, He'll start doing a lot of hard things to me." That is like almost being in love, but not quite, because once you are—even if there is a small voice (or some small words: for better, worse, richer, poorer, sickness, health), you throw yourself into it with the conviction that love will make these things easy. And *spiritual* love does—that is where physical love is supposed to lead us. That is why it is no exaggeration at all to say that, for all its physical form, marriage is a spiritual life.

Now spiritual growth depends on a lot of different things. It depends on prayer, vocal and mental, on meditation and contemplation, on attendance at Mass and the Sacraments, on spiritual reading, and particularly on a variety of forms of doing violence to one's self. And all these things are necessary to the development of anyone's spiritual life, no matter what his vocation. *But* the means to these things differ widely, and are governed by the mold of each vocation, and in no vocation, I am sure, is the spiritual life molded by things so much of the earth, earthy, as in marriage. The odor of sanctity, in marriage, is a distinct odor all its own—and only God could recognize it as such. To most ordinary noses it is a trying combination of burned toast and tobacco smoke and cooked cabbage and diaper pails, and a lot of other things too numerous and ridiculous to mention, with nothing whatsoever to indicate to the innocent bystander that these are the means to sanctification. Fasts and penances may be the way for the religious, and ministering to God's poor for the rich, preaching God's Word and performing God's Sacraments for the clergy, but for the married, it is embracing what is there to be done within the four walls of their home.

Take my good and noble husband, for instance, and the matter of mortification. Little did he, a man of delicate tastes and even more delicate digestion, realize that when he took unto himself a wife she would present him in no time at all with an array of children who, God be praised, would be fine and healthy and need their pants changed often. Nor would she rest there, but having decided to keep children, she must also decide to keep goats. However, never let it be said that the Lord is stingy with grace. My husband has met and conquered in the struggle with the concupiscence of the senses. His nose is at last mortified.

But it does not end there. Having become perfectly detached in the matter of what's in the breeze, this trial is exchanged for another which might be called "What's in a squeeze?" It all looked so providential at the time. The way the rider turned up, working the same shift, living on the same route—God shows His love in even the smallest things, we said, like figuring out a way to pay some of the expenses on the car. Ah yes—and whom the Lord loveth, He chastiseth! So the providentially dis-covered rider turns out to be a man who sucks oranges! And into the furnace for Newland—this time it's his ears. Have you ever driven mile after mile in the dead of night sitting beside a man who squeezes and sucks oranges? "Darling," I said, "offer it up."

"Brother—don't think I don't!"

I have a pretty pamphlet in front of me now, with oodles of rules in it for the Christian married, and aside from the dogmas it repeats, the burden of success seems to rest on being clean and neat and dressing for dinner. Maybe we're screwy—but I can't say I have ever meas-ured an upsurge of love for my mate at the sight of his freshly shaved chin. However, I have sat in the kitchen at one-thirty in the morning waiting for him to get home from work, and I have loved him more, whiskers and dirty shirt and all, because for the sake of our children and myself, he has put up once more with forty-five minutes with an orange-sucker.

So much for mortification, only one of the ingredients of the spiritual life. Next, at random, take silence. Silence for the married would seem to be impossible. You've got to talk to each other. But it has its place—and that is in refusing to quarrel. One of the first disagreements to raise its head in our married life had to do with where to sit in church. My husband was brought up sitting in the middle. I was brought up sitting in the front. He, no matter how hard he tried, could not relax and pray in the front—he was overwhelmed by a sense of being on public display. I tried sitting in the middle, and Mass became a kind of on-again-off-again peep show, which I attended while doing a lady-like buck-and-wing. I peeked to the

N

left, I peered to the right, I saw the Ordinary through this lady's veil, and the Canon over that lady's feathers. It was exhausting and distracting and completely unsatisfactory. I should add that Bill is over six feet tall and hats are no distraction for him. So sooner or later—I hate to admit it—we had words over it. How could he persist in sitting in the middle when I couldn't sit anywhere but in the front? And why didn't he want to sit in the front? It was only a matter of getting used to it—and if he loved God enough, surely he would want to sit in the front. Now this last doesn't follow at all, and it's a good thing all the people who do love God don't want to sit in the front—there are only two front pews. But no— he was adamant. He could not pray in the front. He had a suggestion. Why didn't he continue to sit in the middle, and I continue to sit in the front? I was horrified—this was *awful!* We were *married,* we were supposed to be doing these things *together.* It all indicated, to me, something terribly wrong, and I plagued him unmercifully, with melancholy sighs and broad hints and the wrong kind of silence every Sunday after Mass. He, on the contrary, practised the right kind of silence and never rose to the bait. And then, one day, I overheard two women discussing us, with relish and licking their chops. ". . . and you know what? They never sit together at Mass! She sits in the front, and he sits in the back. I wonder why???" And I howled; the whole thing was too ridiculous and they'd never have believed the truth if I'd told them. From the gleam in their eyes I could tell they suspected all kinds of things—ultimately that we had separate bedrooms, I'm sure. I'd given a good imitation of a nagging wife, and all for a difference in pews. Better to have kept the peace and accepted hi very good reasons for sitting where he must, and waited for God to level the mountains and fill the valleys of our life together. As He has—in this regard. He has sent us a batch of children who *have* to sit in the front— they're really too short to sit in the middle. And my spouse faithfully escorts them up there every Sunday morning. Me? Do I now enjoy Mass in a spirit of deep recollection? Not at all—I'm busy keeping track of my children.

Then there is the matter of prayer. Spirituality is dependent on prayer, so for the married there must be much prayer. But one of the exasperating things about married life, after it is under way and the family begins to grow, is that there isn't too much time for prayer— at least vocal prayer. So prayer, in the main, must be for the married, mental prayer—that running conversation with God which is so easy but seems to be, for far too many, shrouded in mystery—if indeed they have heard of it at all. That is something I don't understand, and don't propose to waste time trying to figure out here. But I certainly think the news should be shouted from the housetops. Mental prayer is so simple it's absurd— "lifting the heart and the mind to God." It's really, I think, the easiest form of prayer, and it's natural for the married. In times of crisis, whether they know it or not, people will use it instinctively. Like a mother who is frantic, looking for her child, "Please, God, please, don't let him be lost." Why wait till then to start having your own kind of conversation with God? You can do it all day long, whenever you're not having conversation with others. You find out after a while that it is so sweet that you'll begin to cut down on your conversations with others—unnecessary conversations. And when you can't employ mental prayer, you can employ whatever you are doing at the time as prayer. Contrarily enough, the more difficult a thing is to do, the more eloquent a prayer it makes. And it's surprising the number of things that will cease to be difficult once they have become prayer.

Then there is penance—another required subject in the pursuit of the spiritual life; and again, marriage is bursting with opportunities. In regard to penance, I am conducting a crusade—and to no avail at all—against hand lotions. All the propaganda put out by the makers and sellers of hand lotions makes me violently ill. Hand lotions will make or break the marriage, they shout. Ha! Hand lotions will make or break the makers of hand lotion—and no one else. Your husband will hate your raw red hands, they insist. Whose husband? Not mine. I don't hate the sight of his hands, up to and above his wrists, hanging out of the too short sleeves of a jacket he's been wearing for years. Certainly it hurts his pride, but it serves as a very good penance. I don't think, when I see them, "How horrible—so ill-fitting." They are more usefully occupied, even when they are just hanging limp, than a lot of hands in a lot of nicely tailored sleeves. And he doesn't think, when he sees my red hands in winter, "Disgusting—love is out the window." Of course if he did, I wouldn't do it—I'd even succumb to using the hand lotions, because one of the things a woman must do for her husband is try to look the way he wants her to look. But my husband happens to think that when Our Lady warned *Do Penance*—she meant penance. And if it's hand lotions versus penance, "then on you, honey, penance looks good." Before anyone gets the idea that I'm trying to paint a picture of us that is too-too noble, let me hasten to remind them that the idea isn't original with us. The whole idea originated with Jesus (and He was doing it for us). With Him it wasn't too-short sleeves, or chapped skin, with Him it was nails.

And all this brings us to poverty. There are vocations within vocations, if that makes sense, and it is easy to see them in marriage. For instance, some families' vocation is poverty—and the wolf is hanging around the door, on and off, all their life long. With other families, it's sickness, and they have periodic brushes with death all their life long. For some, it's public scandal, and for others it's wealth—with the contingent obligation to provide for the poor. All of them lead souls to God, only along different paths. With us, up to now, it's been poverty; Holy Church makes us hopeful when she calls it "holy poverty."

It's not like the poverty of the religious—we took no special vow, except that "richer-poorer" part of the marriage vow. So I can't truthfully say that we embraced holy poverty. Rather, holy poverty embraced us. There was no doubt God wanted her to embrace us. At the time, you don't see too clearly why—except that it's His will and you pray for the grace to love it. Afterwards you can look back and see very clearly why—a lot of reasons why—but outstanding among them all is this: that it takes trial to teach you to love each other spiritually, trial to teach you to love God—and most of all, trial to teach you how God loves you. Isn't it a paradox?

One of the things that makes it difficult to adjust to poverty, even the idea of poverty, is that poverty is so embarrassing. This is not an age that sees Christ in the poor, and poverty never looks providential, just improvi-

dent. And the first step along the path is to do a general
housecleaning in the matter of values; it helps to have
the Gospels in hand. That was where our values had got
themselves distorted. We had a fair-to-middling acquaint-
ance with what Christ said in the Gospels, but having
never been pushed to apply it much, it was so much
pretty poetry. "Consider the lilies of the field" had
never moved us to the point of ecstasy. But when the
screws begin to tighten, one is apt to go rushing about
looking for answers. We prayed like mad, and it had no
effect on the onrushing poverty. We tried to "help ourselves"—after all, God helps those, etc. But to no avail.
We kept a stiff upper lip, and a brave front before our
family and friends. All it seemed, from both inside and
out, was that we weren't smart enough, didn't know the
right angles, or if we did, hadn't tried them. Nothing
ventured, nothing gained, so we ventured the right
angles. And poverty crept closer and closer.

And then one night—as usual, searching Scripture for
the answers—a text we had read and heard many times
before jumped right off the printed page and hit us
between the eyes. "Your Father knows your needs before
you tell Him." Such relief, with that! Of course He knew,
so knowing we were growing shorter and shorter of
funds, and had so many needs, surely tomorrow He
would start to provide for them. But tomorrow, and
tomorrow, and tomorrow, He did *not* provide for them,
and then the truth began slowly to dawn. Maybe we had
other needs, and they were more important—and poverty was His way of providing for them. It was a frighten-
ing prospect, awaiting God's good time. We had no
choice but to wait. He simply did nothing about the
poverty, at least nothing in the material sense. But grace

is always at work, and slowly the thing began to taste sweet. If anyone had told either of us that waiting hour by hour for the food to put in our children's mouths would be sweet, we'd have assured them they were mad. But that is what happens. He levelled us right to the ground by refusing to bless our own efforts with success, and then He showed us the bare palm of His hand by feeding us through the efforts of others. People we have never even met, known only by their names at the end of a letter, fed us in the name of Christ. Humility is hard to come by, and when it does you've got to be good to hang on to it. I hesitate to say we are humble because we have been poor—but at least we know what humility is. For such stubborn flesh as we, it is not a lesson one learns by choice, but by force. We would have had to be incredibly blind not to see it. "Of yourself, you are nothing." Most people have to struggle to understand it, and are at a loss to define it. But to the poor, God says, "Look, I'll show you." Nothing, nothing, nothing—everything we did came to nothing—but out of His love He provided for us through the love of others. Our families, our friends, and as I said, people we did not even know—but nothing came of our own efforts.

And there was another aspect of humility held up to the light for us—even baser, in the eyes of most people, than having to live on the alms of others: humiliation. To be thought a fool, a flop, a dead-beat. Brothers and sisters, that's hard to take! It's crammed down your throat until you choke on it, and then slowly you begin to develop the God's-eye-view. Especially the God's-eye-view of each other. Then you look past the familiar face and into the soul, and you understand what it means— to love spiritually. It's not the whole of it, but all you can bear at the moment. "This child is set for the fall, and for the resurrection . . . and for a sign which shall be *contradicted*." How the Cross scandalizes the world! It's such a contradiction. It contradicts all the rules for success and happiness all the experts can cook up. Here, in contradiction, was love really beginning to bloom! Now it made the best sense it had ever made: "She is flesh of his flesh, and bone of his bone." If the married really want to understand what it means, then let them welcome trials—nay, run to meet them. They come with commensurate grace, and grace over, and grace above, and grace until it spills over—and because grace is the gift of Love, if it is used, it begets love. We were no different from a thousand, a million, other couples who had been given a taste of poverty, or suffering, or whatever cross He chose to send, and we had thought all along that we loved each other. You don't begin to know what love is until you see your beloved suffer. Then, at last you understand. *Marriage is a spiritual union.* Then you love not just with your heart, but with your soul.

And there is one more (not one—a thousand, but this has to end somewhere!) ingredient in a recipe for spirituality for the married, and that is the children. They are the final proof, the incarnation, of the spiritual union. Let the physiologists wag their heads at such naiveté as this—and insist they are merely the result of a union in flesh. Pray for them because they do not know immortality when they see it. What a vocation marriage is! To be called to co-operate with Almighty God and have a part in His image and likeness. As Saint Paul could write, "Christ is glorified in my body," so too can the married. In my body, and of my body, and through my body—and when the union of two brings forth one, and three, and five, and more—He is glorified again and again. Now understand the term "lay priests," who bring forth other Christs in a union so unreasonable that Coventry Patmore wrote of it that it is not unlike the Transubstantiation—wherein bread remains bread and wine remains wine, and the two become Christ. A man remains a man, and woman a woman, and Christ says the "two become one flesh." We are so used to seeing children that we do not consider the miracle that they are. The whole thing is above reason. Marriage is a spiritual life which blossoms with immortality.

It occurs to me that perhaps this whole thing smacks of the too-good-to-be-true. Is there no dissonance anywhere? Is this whole thing, for the Newlands, one long unending emotional and spiritual binge? No, it is not. But I do not intend to scandalize our public or our children by baring our feet of clay. It is enough to say we have them. Have we never awakened one not-so-fine morning and asked ourselves: "How did I get here?" Many times—and we've thrashed around and toyed with the idea that the whole thing was a big mistake in the first place. But—and this is my own private theory, it's possible I could be wrong—marriage is no mistake. Marriage *is*. It involves a gamble, a risk, and a good or a bad choice, but once a marriage is made, it's *the* way to God. He wants us—and He will have us, if only we will have Him. If I were to be limited to one rule on spirituality for the married, it would be to remember that no matter how tough it can be, how lonely at times, how unhappy, it can never be a solo flight—you've got to do it together.

AN INTERRACIAL CATHOLIC MARRIAGE

∽

NANCY GRENELL DU BOIS

MY HUSBAND AND I met at an interracial settlement house in Harlem where I worked. He had just received his discharge from the Army after spending a year in Australia and in a hospital in Texas. He is a West Indian by birth—his father having been a redheaded Frenchman and his mother a brown-skinned woman. I am an American—of French, English and Irish descent. I liked interracial work immensely. I loved working with the poor and I felt completely "dedicated" to the cause of serving God through serving Interracial Justice. It really was something to put your teeth into, and every day was a challenge. The young people I worked with were sincere, loyal, trustworthy, and loving God with a selflessness and intensity far greater than that of most young Catholics I had previously met.

But the way of a man with a maid is the way of a man with a maid, and it wasn't many months before I realized that perhaps I wasn't as completely "dedicated" as I thought I was. When he first asked me to marry him, I said No indeed. My life was set in its permanent pattern. How little I knew!

How little I knew also what a furore would be raised by the idea of our getting married! From those from whom I expected the most understanding and love, I received the least. I was called on the phone by the president of my former Catholic college and told that she wanted to put in her protest before it was too late. I was told a sad, long story by a monsignor whom I consulted, about an Italian-Irish marriage that turned out badly because of different "races." I was told by another priest that while marriage is a personal affair, it couldn't possibly turn out well because of our different backgrounds. I was warned I would have to spend the rest of my life in the black ghettos of America. I was warned I could never travel again. I was warned that if God did bless (?) our marriage with children, they were doomed to untold misery. I was told that I would ruin my family. I was told that I was ignorant, stupid, selfish . . . that while the Church did not prohibit such marriages, I might very well retard the work of Interracial Catholic Justice by many years. I was told by a dear friend that I was fifty years too soon. I was told that I would probably kill my mother, my only living parent. There was much more said against our prospective marriage, and it all weighed very heavily on my soul. I had many weeks of anxious prayer and just plain old worry. Above all, I didn't want our marriage to hurt the work of Interracial Justice or the sincere and marvellous efforts of those associated with us.

However, in time I grew peaceful again and felt certain that God approved of our marriage, even though others didn't, and in the autumn of 1944 we were married with five priests on the altar and a lot of friends in the pews.

188 BE NOT SOLICITOUS

While I had a lot of criticism about the marriage, I also had a lot of heartening encouragement. From most of my young associates I received only love and warm encouragement. They were willing to stand by us, no matter what the outcome, and I shall always cherish them for their trust and faith, and I shall never, never forget the great service they did me at a time when I was sorely distressed.

And also, after seven years, being more mature and, I trust, wiser, I can see that much of the criticism came because my friends loved me and did not want me to get hurt. It wasn't malicious, and any bitterness of hurt that I felt has long since gone. We have also been apologized to for the things said at that time, and it takes a big person to admit that he was wrong. We also had some wonderfully Christian letters from friends and even strangers, from other countries as well as this one.

My husband wavered not at all during our engagement. He remained steadfast and firm in his conviction that this was the marriage for him (and accordingly for me!), and that since God, using the Church as His voice, did not oppose it, what others felt and said was their business, not ours.

His judgment proved sound. God has blessed our marriage (no question-mark this time) with attractive, intelligent children, and we share a love and companionship that has grown with the years.

Now to take up various aspects of Interracial Marriage about which there are usually questions—the reaction of families and friends, the position of children, etc. I can only write of my own experience, as this is the only marriage I have ever contracted, or ever expect to. My husband has been an orphan since he was six years old, so there was no question of my being accepted or rejected by his family. I have a mother living a couple of thousand miles away. She is not a Catholic and has never really been agreeable to the fact that I became one when I was nineteen. She had never known any Negroes except those who worked in the house for her. She is intelligent, kindly, and Christian. But she accepts the mores and distinctions of her social class without probing as to the why and wherefores. She has never deviated from the pattern in which she was raised, and her eyebrows go up when those of others do. She is not consciously anti-Jew, anti-Negro or anti-anything. She was raised, and then raised her family, in the typical middle-class, well-to-do American pattern, where daughters marry professional men and sons become successful professional or business men.

When I wrote to her of my forthcoming marriage she was naturally shocked and horrified: with her background you couldn't expect anything else. But she bowed to the inevitable at last and accepted it well, considering. She first visited us when our eldest son was nine months old and our second child well on the way. She said she came to spend one night; she remained two weeks. And when she left she kissed my husband goodbye and told me that we had the happiest home she had ever been in. She showed the same tenderness toward her little golden-skinned, brown-eyed grandson as she does now to another grandson, my sister's child, who is blond and blue-eyed. This great change was mainly due to my husband's patient and intelligent re-education of her way of thinking. Their discussions were long and deep. The rest of it sprang from the fact that we do, through the goodness of God, have such a happy home that she was bound to feel and see it. She didn't, as she had feared, find her daughter weighed down with the misery of a misalliance, but a happy mother and wife with good friends, a cheerful apartment and lots to occupy her. Since that visit, we've had no more complaints about our marriage. Not that she approves one hundred percent or ever will, but she doesn't disapprove completely either. And in this life, I've learned, that is a great deal to be grateful for. Our letters are always loving and intimate. So much for Mother.

I don't know how many friends my husband lost by marrying me, because he has never said. I made a couple of "enemies" among his friends—female ones, because he *is* a handsome guy, and they had their eyes on him. I don't blame them either. And there have been so many white women marrying colored men in the last ten years that a natural resentment has sprung up among colored women. For myself, I am conscious of losing just one friend—a pleasant girl whom I liked very much. She had been helping in interracial work herself when I first knew her, but apparently carrying interracial relations into marriage was too much for her. I've never heard from her since. Oddly enough, those of my friends whom I knew before I ever went to work in Harlem, before I was even remotely interested in interracial things, have never criticized my marriage. I fully expected to lose some of them. I have a close friend who lives in California. She visited us shortly after our second baby arrived. There are only two Negro families in the town she lives in, and her knowledge of such matters is at least hazy. She accepted my husband just as though he were Bill Jones, the boy next door. Maybe that is just being a superb friend. I don't know. Anyway it is good enough for me. Through our marriage we have made some new friends, as well as having kept ninety-nine percent of the old ones. I'm satisfied—and grateful, both to God and to them. Friends are a necessary part of a well-rounded life.

One of the BIG arguments against Interracial Marriage, which I have heard over and over again, is that the children of such a union will suffer. We have had at least half a dozen interracial couples contemplating marriage come to see us since we were married. Most of them were sent by priests. And the question of children always seems to worry them a lot. Our oldest boy is only six, so I can't judge yet how much our children will suffer because they were born of a mixed racial union, but I am of the same opinion as I was at first. And that is —not very much, for they are children of a happy home. Catholic children are trained to obedience, trained to love God and their fellow men, trained to put first things first. They will suffer, but that is part of living in an imperfect world. Our oldest son, who is in the first grade at the parochial school, asked me recently if he were "colored." I told him he was. He was very pleased. In his school, out of over five hundred students there are only about five colored children. One day, when I was visiting the school, one of his "pals" (a favorite word apparently among that age group) asked me if my son were colored. I, of course, said "Yes." He looked at him closely, then said: "Are you his mother?" I replied in the affirmative. Then he said: "Go on, he's just tanned!" Now how would you answer that?

Yes, my son is colored, and in America that means a second-rate citizen. But not in the eyes of God. And we hope to give him the self-respect and wisdom to understand that the opinion of the majority is not necessarily the correct opinion. That it depends on him, and above all on his trust in God, and his understanding of human frailty. No one in his right mind could look at my son's father and say he is second-rate anything. His skin is brown, and his mind, his soul and his heart are of a quality that need no apology. What the future holds for my children only God knows. That is rather trite. Also, that they will get out of life what they put into it—and that is trite too. Their parents will try to make them good Catholics, good citizens and good in the job they are meant for. We do not believe they are more handicapped than other children, in fact far less than millions in the world today.

I would not get on a platform and advocate Interracial Marriage for anyone. Marriage is between two people—and God—and does not concern others. But neither would I discourage it as such. The problems of Interracial Marriage are like the problems of any marriage: each has its own. In any relation certain aspects are enlarged; others minimized. Until recently we lived in a large city, and city people are notorious for leaving their neighbors alone. Little scandalizes in a metropolitan area. Now we live in a small town and are, I believe, the only interracial couple here. So far no one has put any flaming crosses on our lawn, nor do we expect them to. We have heard that our neighbors across the road call us "Niggers," but we also heard that they called the people we bought the house from "Wops." There are always such folk in the world. They do not hurt us, but should remind us ourselves to grow in tolerance. To some people an Englishman is a "Limey" and the Irish are "Micks." I suppose it gives a sense of superiority to belittle others.

In conclusion—but actually, what "conclusion" can there be, since this is life going on, day by day, for a man and his wife and his children? It is possible, however, to conclude that perhaps God plans such marriages, and blesses them, because in His infinite wisdom, He uses such unions to teach those of His children who are stubborn that we *all* are His children, regardless of color. What God has joined together—my brown-skinned husband and me—let no one put asunder.

o

THE JOY OF POVERTY

~~·~~

"MRS. J."

Editor's Note: This story came from Integrity. *Ed Willock and Carol Jackson had written asking a friend who was expecting her fifth baby to send them "a simple statement of her attitude towards the poverty she had known so intimately." They put in a five-dollar bill in case she was short at the moment. The story is her answer.*

DEAR CAROL AND ED,

Thank you ever so much for the five dollars. It's like this. Bill did get a job, shortly after I wrote that letter chiding you on your "half-baked" praying. This time you hit the jackpot. Two weeks ago he got a job at seventy-five dollars. Several nights ago the bosses in a club where he used to work called us from New York and asked Bill to come back to work for them. He used to be just one of the players in the band there. This time they want him to get a band together and be the leader. They're giving him one hundred dollars. So in about two weeks he'll be there—or at least that is how it looks *now*. I'm stunned and haven't quite digested it. Although I shouldn't be surprised at what God does

But He always does so much *more* than I expect. The seventy-five was okay with me, but the hundred is rather breath-taking.

However, that's getting away from the five dollars. So Bill is working, but naturally it's taking almost every penny of his wages to pay our bills. We owe so much to so many, we just don't know which to pay first. And last week it was the mortgage and taxes payment at sixty-four dollars, and when you figure Bill's gasoline money for each day, it left very little for food. I bought a bag of whole wheat flour, some beans, a dozen eggs, two boxes of powdered skimmed milk, and five pounds of stew beef at 19¢ per. We had an adequate (it would seem) diet of oatmeal with powdered milk, homemade bread, and a variety of beef meals: beef stew, vegetable soup with beef, braised beef with baked beans, beef barbecue with beans, and so forth.

Considering that not so long ago we were subsisting on oatmeal and potatoes, this was sumptuous fare. However, my stomach has been in outright rebellion for weeks. I feel it working into knots every time I cook those meals. The spicy smells of the barbecues and baked beans made it reel. A few mouthfuls of oatmeal, and that skimmed milk gets like chalk in my throat, and if I finally force it down, it doesn't stay put anyhow. The whole wheat flour is altogether too rich. Even half white, half whole wheat wouldn't stay, so rather than ruin any more good grain by mixing that useless white flour with it I stopped even trying to eat bread.

As a result I keep getting hungrier and the knots in my stomach get tighter. And all these weeks I've been thinking, "If only I had roast chicken with gravy and cranberry sauce and a glass of whole milk . . ."

Sounds silly, doesn't it? And every time I'd read an

article or see a picture of the starving children of Europe and elsewhere I'd feel so ashamed of myself. But I kept on wanting it. And then I started wishing out loud. At every meal I'd say to Bill, "If only this were roast chicken with gravy . . ." Last week Bill said, "Wait till next payday—even if we have to let some bill wait, we'll have a chicken dinner on Tuesday" (that would have been today).

So I kept on cooking meals, and all the time those smells (which were really good smells) were a torture to me and actually gave me pains in my stomach. And I'd say to myself, "Tuesday—wait until Tuesday."

The funniest part of it all is that I don't ordinarily care about food. I mean, I eat because we have to live, but one thing has always been as good as another to me. And why it had to be chicken?

Saturday morning I woke up with the worst gnawing pains, and I lay there just wanting chicken with gravy and cranberry sauce, and I knew I couldn't stand it any longer.

While I cooked the breakfast oatmeal, I thought, "Today I will have that dinner, because I must have it today. How will it come? Bill has only a dollar to hold him till payday and he needs it all for gas. Then my folks will come out with chicken . . . but no, that won't do, the house is a mess. I don't want anyone to come out today. It's awful and I'm too sick and tired to clean up. Then how? A check—that's it! Some manuscript . . ."

So I watched for the mailman while the children ate their oatmeal—and the way they eat bowls of that stuf and love it is astounding. The mailman came earlie that day, bless his heart. I ran out to the box and I looke over the envelopes. Nothing in the way of money.

fingered the *Integrity* envelope: thick, too thick for just a letter; not an advertisement, that was *last* month. Why, it must be an appeal for money. Saint Joseph's Feast coming up. People who never ask at other times will beg in March. So I put it down again, thinking, "I'll send them a dollar in two weeks. I'll be able to give *that* much by then." I went back into the kitchen to get more beef out of the freezer and start a meal so it would be ready by noon, put the beans in the oven, then brought out the rest of the mail to read. I was standing over that steaming, stewing beef in a mild agony with the unwanted aroma assailing my nostrils when I opened your letter and the five-dollar bill slid right into my hands. I hate to sound irreverent, but do you recall all those times in the Bible—or it seemed like a lot of times—a dove would circle over Our Lord and a Voice would be heard saying, "This is My Beloved Son in Whom I am well pleased"?

My head was spinning, I was so happy. Isn't God good? He doesn't mind how silly you are. He gives you things like this. Surely I must be the most spoiled child in the world. I have the most indulgent Father.

I can't even think about poverty any more without becoming joyful. And although I say these things to a few close friends who might be sympathetic to such ideas, I hesitate to make any public statements on the matter for fear of giving scandal.

Won't they be shocked to hear that I am enamored of poverty and insecurity? How can people approve when we go on having babies every year or two and yet never know from day to day or from week to week what our financial status will be?

And wasn't it a foolhardy thing, not so many weeks

ago, when we had no money and were suffering the effects of months of unemployment, that I should have dared to pray that Bill would not take a certain job open for him? What kind of a job? Civil Service with a steady income, sick-leave pay, vacation with pay, pension, and an opportunity for advancement—and only a walk from our house. All the thoughts that ran through our minds. Did it not seem providential that of all the places we went to live, we should have come here, so close to those government buildings? And wasn't it better than commuting? And wasn't it the *sensible* thing to do? And surely the Church has always taught in her social dogmas that these are things men should have, especially *family* men. It certainly would have brought peace to the hearts of our many friends and relatives who were anxiously "sweating out" this unemployment spell with us. It was always the shadow of insecurity hanging over us that troubled those who love us. They didn't mind the ever growing family, but they would say, "If only he had a *steady* job. If only he'd get out of *that* line and into something secure."

And there came a day he said, "I've made up my mind. I've got to take that job. Things can't go on like this any longer. We can't exist on unemployment insurance and I can't see my family starve . . . ."

So it was decided. And we just sat there not daring to say any more about it. And I felt a kind of sorrow coming over me. From now on we would have a regular, certain income. All we had to do was to sit down and work out a budget, and for all the years ahead there would always be that money, and life could be planned and set. No financial worries, no uncertainties.

But (and here is where my talk grows scandalous) n

more surprises, no more unexpected incidents. We had had no security but divine security, a complete, all-abiding confidence in God. He would always provide. No matter what earthly and temporal forces played upon our lives He would supersede them. If we just kept doing our best, and just held tightly to His hand, He'd always be with us. But now we were to have a new kind or security, a prosaic, earthly kind. Ah well, perhaps this was the way He meant it to be. Perhaps He was saying, "Time the game was ended. You've had enough now of thrills and adventure and excitement in your quest for your daily bread. Now settle down and take it this way." Yes, it could be that this job was God's Will for us. I wanted to be a good sport about it and sensible and even thankful ("thank God for *everything*," you know) but I couldn't help murmuring heavenwards, not a complaint, just a reminder, "But it won't be as much *fun* this way."

And then the telephone rang and Bill reached over and lifted the instrument. "It's Charlie. He has a job for me, two days a week." I said, "Take it, take it. One job leads to another. It will work out. Say 'Yes'!"

And he said "yes." The safe, sane, earthly wall of security gave way and the sadness went with it. There was nothing left to sustain us but God. We suddenly felt light-hearted and happy again.

It isn't that we believe everyone should turn down steady jobs, regular employment, temporal security. On the contrary, we approve of all those blessings and pray that God will be bountiful to all our hard-working brothers and sisters in Christ.

It's just that we feel that God must have meant otherwise for us. And that is a big broad statement to make, but it's true, that the times we are happiest are the times when we are not sure of anything except the fact that God is our Father and He loves us and takes a special interest in our affairs, and He always gives us whatever we need or *should have* and sometimes even foolish little unimportant things we don't actually have to have but would like.

Oh yes, I know we are not privileged characters partaking of His generosity. He loves *all* His children and does as much for any of them. But with us it seems to be in our nature to live in *absolute dependence* on Him. And the only thing that can keep us absolutely dependent on His loving care is to be without earthly security.

Do you shake your head in disapproval? Are we scandalizing you? Are all those who have rushed to our assistance over this, that and the other thing, thinking, "Why, the beggars! And not even ashamed! And saying they wouldn't have it otherwise?"

Don't blame us too hastily. Maybe it has to be so for our own personal sanctification and eventual salvation. After all, there are some people who never go to church unless there's sickness or trouble in the home. And maybe that's why God sends them periodic sicknesses and troubles. He's got to get His children to Him somehow, and if that's the only thing that will bring them . . . well? And perhaps we are the kind who would grow forgetful about Him if we had a lifetime guarantee of temporal blessings. So He keeps us with no hope, no promise, nothing—but Divine Providence. With some people you have to do things the hard way.

Strangely enough, having nothing but Him, we know a light-heartedness and joy in living that far outweighs all the little everyday troubles and upsets in our lives. And now we know why Saint Francis enjoyed his married life, being wedded to Lady Poverty. And we know why the highways and byways and all the Italian countryside echoed his songs and rang with his laughter.

It wasn't always this way with us, nor did this living under the Will of God come about overnight. When we married we were much like any other couple of our world. The war was on and Bill in the service, expecting to transfer out of the city at any time. We had rented a very lovely two-room apartment in one of the prettiest parts of Brooklyn. The rent was high, but I was still a career girl and my salary could handle it. No one expected an ordinary seaman to have that kind of money. Babies? We had considered all that before marriage. We were Catholics and knew the teaching of the Church: no birth control. But more than that, we wanted children. We were a curious mixture of the self-sufficient, independent pagan and the loyal-to-our-tenets Catholic. It was all settled. We would have nine children, one every two years. That would get them all in before I hit forty.

I still get a little wide-eyed now when I look back on our naive assumption that you could have babies to order much like a spaghetti dinner in a restaurant. That was the pagan in us.

How would it be done? By means of Rhythm, of course. The safe and sane compromise between the world's way and the—let's call it—the difficult, unthinkable, any other way. That was the Catholic in us.

We had a twinge of conscience about it. There was a lease to be signed and we knew I couldn't work and have a baby too. We consulted a priest. Would it be all right to practise Rhythm for one year, and spend that year in the apartment? It sounds awfully silly now, but that place was home to me from the first moment I set eye on it, and it was a very precious thing and more tangible than a baby which had not been seen yet, and anyhow there were going to be *nine* children. He did a very wise thing, that priest. He might have said, "No, don't take the apartment. You've got to leave things up to God and take your chances." And we would have obeyed, but the psychological effects might have impeded the flow of grace coming our way. Instead he said, "If the place means so much to you, rent it. But just remember *no sin* in your marriage. Don't commit any sin . . . Oh, and I wouldn't advise you to sign any lease."

So we went back relieved and thoroughly happy, and signed the lease anyhow because I figured if we did have a baby we'd leave and they wouldn't hold us to the contract because babies are an act of God.

We were happy there. The place had something about it that made us happy. It wasn't only the marriage, it was the home. And it was home to us from the start. After you're in such an atmosphere, happy together, growing together in the way that Christian marriage inspires a man and wife, you act upon the grace of God. And there's where the baby came in. We would talk about our "children" often. Sooner or later the thought had to force itself: supposing we never have any? That led to, "How do we even know we could have one?" "Supposing I became pregnant, how could anyone even say if the baby would live?" Then that baby loomed more important than the beloved apartment, and it would seem that even if we had to sacrifice our home, we must know if we could have a baby. Finis Rhythm.

Several months later we moved out of our happy

home. There was no arguing the point, a baby was infinitely better than an apartment. But that didn't stop me from shedding bitter tears at the leave-taking. And no place ever after was quite like it, and perhaps there never again will be one quite so perfect this side of heaven.

Our next stop was a housing project close to the Brooklyn Navy Yard. It would have been hard to find a greater contrast. But we were glad to have a place of our own. Those were months of never-ending sickness, days and nights of nausea. And in between sick spells I budgeted the fifty dollars a month allotment and whatever cash Bill brought in besides. We bought our furniture piece by piece. But relatives bought the bedroom set and kitchen set. Until the chairs and table arrived—and in those days you really waited for furniture delivery—we used the beds for chairs and set up a suitcase between them for a table. There was much to be done in the way of putting up curtains and covering the floors —and Bill came home on twelve-hour passes or weekend liberty. It was a hectic existence and not easy, but we were happy through it all and we had begun to witness the first manifestations of Divine Providence. It was the way an insurmountable obstacle would be overcome, the way an urgent debt would be paid by an unexpected gift of money. And there was something not quite credible in the way the little we had took care of so much. There didn't seem to be a real proportion between income and outgo, and after a time we just figured it had something to do with God looking after us and let it go at that.

The main thing upon which our lives centered was the baby. And we were brought closer than ever by this

new tie. Our spiritual development was another blessing. From the start we had been frequent, almost daily,
communicants. There was a chapel and Catholic priest
at Bill's base, so even when he was not at home he was
able to attend Mass in the morning. We had married in
the month of March, so had placed our marriage under
the patronage of Saint Joseph and had begun a novena
to him to prepare for his feastday. We said our prayers
together and followed a kind of liturgy in living without
quite realizing it. For each month is dedicated to a
special saint or occasion, and we continued including
novenas in our daily prayers: June for the Sacred Heart;
July, the Precious Blood, and so on. There was no reason
to presume before marriage that things would go this
way. We were religious to an extent, but this was really
extraordinary. You will have to take my word for it. It
was something new and unusual, and we never actually
thought about what we were doing from an objective
viewpoint. Prayer marked our days and filled our life,
and it came about as naturally as eating and sleeping.
Afterwards when I thought back on that first year, I
came to see that there is absolutely no limit to the graces
God pours down on married people. They have only to
receive and correspond to them. It seemed to have begun
with the taking of vows and the Nuptial Mass. How God
must love every bride and groom and bless especially
the marriage that is "marriage in Christ"!

A few weeks after our first wedding anniversary our
son was born. The next day Bill was sent south to a base
for commando training.

The birth of the baby actually posed a new problem in
our lives. It had been such a startling and severe ordeal
that I remained weak and sick for long afterwards.
Actually the rest of the family revealed it had not been

a surprise to them, because I had looked so bad all during pregnancy that they had been dreading what might happen at birth. I had been too ill to know how I had looked. They were relieved that the baby and I both survived and took the attitude that "it had better be several years before it happens again."

Bill had been given his share of "after all, if you love her, have some consideration . . . Don't kill the poor girl." He had been thoroughly frightened anyhow, and that kind of talk, which seemed to put all the blame for my pain and suffering directly on him, didn't help him much.

No one said anything to me. They all thought I still looked half dead and had learned a lesson. Frankly, I had only enough strength to concentrate on the big project on hand, breast feeding my son.

There are so many factors that color a life. You could write a novel on one day in a life. There is always more to be left out than can ever be put in the telling.

I have to get right on to the next big incident which bound us more closely to the Divine Will. The letters between Bill and me had considered the pros and cons of another baby. It was hard to find many pros. The first consideration was my health. It had grown worse since the baby's birth, I was alone (because I wanted it so) in the apartment taking care of the baby. Another pregnancy would mean another nine months of invalidism, and someone else would have to care for our son. Finally, it would place a burden on our parents, who would have to assume responsibility for both baby and me, etc., etc. It ceased to be a matter for discussion, however, when one day there arrived a letter from Bill saying he thought it best to take a vow of chastity. In my state of health I should have been relieved at the prospect of no longer going through the ordeal of child-birth. But while I deeply appreciated the spirit of love and self-sacrifice on my husband's part and all for my benefit, it seemed like a negative solution and a running away from the problem. At the first opportunity I hastened over to the Franciscan church on Thirty-first Street, because there confessions are heard all day. I chose not a particular priest but a shorter line.

Only the dear Lord knows the grace and goodness that flow from that church! I had explained the situation quickly and completely. Space does not permit me all that wonderful talk he gave, though I still remember every word of it. He opened my mind and eyes to a broader vista of Christian marriage than I had seen before. Our society prides itself on independence, self-sufficiency, shudders at accepting help from others. He banished the parents' burden idea by explaining God's design in the Christian family, the role our parents play in helping us and what we will do some day for our own children, but best of all the answer that goes beyond Rhythm, planning, abstaining.

"How do *you* know when is the best time to have a baby? Will two years from now be better than next year? Can you foretell the future? *Isn't God wiser than you?* Who should know better than He when a child should be born?" There was more, but the line that climaxed everything for me was, *"Isn't God wiser than you?"*

I went home and knew there were left now only the reasons "for." I wrote Bill, saying we'd better pray for another child, if that were God's Will. It wasn't easy. It was the most difficult decision I have ever made in my life. And I was frightened as I had never been before. It was a fearsome, terrifying thing to do. I who had always planned, figured, calculated carefully, was now putting my whole life into other Hands. It was exactly as though I had been led blindfolded to the edge of a high diving platform and told, "Go ahead, jump. There's water below." I jumped, and landed in the Arms of God. Now I never want to be "on my own" or independent of Him again. Never!

We soon learned how that prayer was answered. The second pregnancy didn't make me an invalid. On the contrary, it seemed to make me stronger, healthier than at any time in my life. The birth was speedy with a minimum of complication. I had never looked better or felt better than the morning Joseph was born. It was the first fruit of reliance on God, and as I held my newborn in my arms that day I thought of the eternal debt of gratitude I owed the Franciscan who gave me the rule for life and living when he asked, "Isn't God wiser than you?" Our son Joseph owes his life to that priest whose name we don't even know.

From that time on our problems were always subordinated to one question: "Is it God's will?" In that we had our answers, made choices, decisions. It's not always easy. Gabriel doesn't drop in each morning with a bulletin saying, "Here's His Will for today." Sometimes you doubt, you question. Sometimes you have all your friends saying prayers and offering Masses that you may be given the light to know and the strength to do. But you have a serene confidence and an unquenchable flame of hope that as long as you are dedicated and consecrated to what He wants, He will not let you go astray and He will direct your life.

MARRIAGE FOR KEEPS

ᕙᕗ

ED WILLOCK

THERE'S A DIFFERENCE between being married and being an expert on marriage. There's a difference between having a group of letters after your name and a group of children at your heels. I'm married, with a group of children. I'm not an expert with a Ph.D. Consequently, in writing about marriage I'll not approach it as a subject but as an experience.

Along with that explanation of the perspective I intend to take, I should add that I am no past-master. My children are not grown up, they are babies and the oldest is eight. We don't know what it would be like to be without an infant in the house. My writing room is not an ivory tower but a kitchen table.

So, there you are. When I speak about children, I'm talking about Mike, Paul, Elizabeth, Ann, Marie, Peter and Clare. Mike breaks windows and says prayers very well. Paul is always smiling, even while he's letting the air out of our neighbor's tires. Ann has the most beautiful eyes for an eight-year-old I have ever seen, but the school examiner tells us she needs glasses. Marie is as shy and as curious as a kitten. She has cheeks like an apple and an appetite like a truck driver. Peter's just beginning to walk, and he looks like Dopey the Dwarf. Clare is the center of attention in her bassinet. Tack their pictures on a wall, against a background of diapers, milk bills, broken toys, worn-out shoes, outgrown overalls, jam-stained doorknobs, broken glass and complaints from the neighbors, and you begin to see marriage as I see it.

But that's only part of the picture. To see the rest, you must see Elizabeth preparing for her bath in the evening: two feet tall and as formidable as Gibraltar. Just to look at her cherubic countenance after we have flushed off a few inches of topsoil subtracted from the back yard, gives a father a feeling of security. Her smile removes any doubt you might have about the bountiful providence of God. And the evening prayers (in spite of the fact that Ann shows off her facility with words and Elizabeth falls asleep) bind every thread of the day together into a pattern of marriage that is convincing. It's here to stay and it's for keeps. It's a way to spend a life. It's a way to God, and that's Heaven all along the route.

That will give you an idea of the way I tackle marriage, but I'm not speaking only for myself. I didn't invent marriage. It has been with us a long time. I see my family as one unit among millions of families. I see it as a long chain of wedding rings extending back through generations, and this tradition goes back to a table at which Christ sat. There was a wedding banquet and the wine ran out. He changed the water into wine. By His presence there, His act of divine generosity, and His sanctification of marriage, He has made the water of marriage into sacramental wine.

P

Christian marriage is like nothing else, least of all like that caricature of marriage—the typical modern thing (which is a kind of legal cohabitation). It isn't a love song sung with "a girl for you, a boy for me, but Heaven help us from having three." It isn't two people making the best of an uncomfortable situation. It is an adventure with Christ.

Along about the last month before the knot is tied, the average fellow begins to bite his finger nails. The girl has taken over, and she's in a sweet swoon about the details. The fellow finds himself in a rapidly moving caravan, dashing by jewelry counters, clothes dummys, flat-to-rent ads, consultation of the bank book, furniture stores, draperies, best man, bridesmaid, and all the little details that the girl sees with uncanny intuition. Looming before him is *one* thing, MARRIED LIFE. It's a big thing! What will it be like? Never mind about details, look at this big, strange unknown!

Most fellows go through that and so did I. With some very tidy arithmetic I had concluded that two could live as cheaply as one and a half. I had a steady job, as jobs go. We could afford my staying away from work a week, have an inexpensive honeymoon, and then get by on bread and water until the first pay day. Of course, we could have grown old apart, instead of together, as so many couples do, waiting until we could *afford* it. "Not for us," said we, and it was clinched!

Marriage was a few weeks away. We hadn't found a place to live. Dorothy lived in one town and I in another. We had decided to set up house in my town. But, as I say, flats (at the rent we could pay) were scarce.

The day I'm describing had been pretty rough. I operated a machine in a small plant. That day, the machine was balky and the stock was bad. I fretted and fumed, my feet itching to be pounding around town, looking for a flat. This one gnawing desire being frustrated discolored my entire picture of the future. I went home on the subway in a blue funk. My mother detected the mood as I played golf with my peas at the supper table. So I put it up to her. "Listen, Mom, we've got plenty of room here. Why can't Dot and I move in here after we're married, and then we can take our time looking for a flat."

I should have known better! My mother was always a lady for calling a spade a spade (and still is, for that matter). I wouldn't have missed it for the world! Her exact words I don't remember, but they went something like this:

"Listen here, Sonny. I prepared you for Baptism about twenty-three years ago. I nursed you, bundled you up and put your booties on. After that, when you were seven I tucked in your shirt and brushed down your cowlick when you went to receive your First Communion. At Confirmation you were twelve, and still helpless. I fixed your necktie, tucked in your shirt and sent you off. But (and here she laid it on) if you think for one minute that Mama is going to lead you down the aisle for Matrimony and home again, you don't know your mother! Matrimony is for men and women, not for children. If you can't handle this problem on your own, probably the simplest problem you'll ever face as a couple, then you may be old enough to marry, but you're not a man!"

In retrospect, her speech added up to this:

A family needs a head, and God designed the man for that role. By nature, the man is aggressive and independent. He works best in the open, free, with liberty to make choices of direction. The woman, on the other hand, achieves her freedom within limits. No matter how valiant she may be, she likes the role of a help-mate to a man of whom she is proud. (A simple little picture that illustrates this point is the fact that in the outdoors, on the plains, in the woods, or behind a plow, a man who is a man, is at home. In such a picture, the woman is dwarfed beside him. As a matter of fact, any woman who does look at home in the great outdoors isn't very feminine. She's likely to have a rasping voice and a horsey look. Just move the couple into a living room and the woman grows in stature. The enclosure reflects her importance.)

Men in our time have not been taking this headship. God forbid that we should return to the tyranny of the Bible-thumping patriarch, but the pendulum is now way over in the other direction. All around us we have seen the way in which men have allowed the brutality of masculine affairs to invade and desecrate the personal environs which the women hold dear.

Wars, the work of men, have ripped the families and slain the children. The economic processes designed by men have depersonalized the worker, prescribed the number of children, turned men into irresponsible pay-checks. The neuroses which characterize our times are the result of this assault upon the heart and sensibilities of society. The women, because of their capacity for generous compassion and the sensitivity that such warm-heartedness engenders, have borne the brunt of this injustice. The intimate personal concern which it is a woman's glory to give, has been disregarded in the masculine madness of money-making, empire building and forensic debate.

Because of that women have difficulty trusting the modern man. Most women still prefer marriage, and they would choose marriage if men assured them a dignified and devoted leadership.

Where this lesson particularly applied in my case and in the case of so many fellows today, is that we tend to reflect rather than remove the woman's fear of insecurity. Instead of providing a shoulder to be wept upon, too many men go to their mothers, girl friends or wives, looking for a hankie. Yes, a man can be gentle, but he can be a gentle-man. He can softly but firmly lead the way out of difficulties, not capitulate to the fears for the future.

It will always be true in marriage that the greatest giving will be on the part of the wife. Through pregnancy and child raising she loses the independence which the man continues to retain. If today the woman is reluctant to do this, it is because she does not trust the man to be loving, confident and considerate when she must of necessity depend solely upon him. We confirm this mistrust whenever we hesitate. A good woman is happy to go through torture for her husband as long as his step is firm, his love tender and his faith strong.

When my mother concluded her sermon, I still wasn't convinced. I know better now, but it takes time to grow up. I just grouched away from the table and sat in the parlour glowering at the design in the carpet. The doorbell rang and my mother passed me a telegram. That telegram gave me the deepest, most gratifying bellylaugh that I have ever had. It isn't easy to explain why it tickled me so much or why I still regard it as one of the most provident lessons that God taught me about marriage. All it said was that it was from Dorothy and would I mind changing the date of the wedding because her Aunt Sarah who lived in Washington had sprained her leg and would not be able to get there as early as we had hoped.

To get the picture you've got to realize that I was looking at that wedding date with the awful expectancy of a condemned prisoner marking off his calendar. Then along comes my beloved and kicks that awe-inspiring date into a cocked hat simply because Aunt Sarah had sprained her leg!

The scales suddenly fell from my eyes and I discovered with a gasp of joy that a woman always has her lovely finger on somebody's pulse, and that means more to her than the C.I.O., the N.A.M., or the U.N., or all combined, especially more than a paltry wedding date.

Take the man who is directing the setting in place of the central span of the Abraham Lincoln bridge. He gets a call from the construction shack. It is his wife on the phone. "I'm sorry to bother you, dear, but would you mind dropping in to the five and dime on the way home and getting some *yellow* paper napkins? It's Uncle George's birthday, and the frosting on the cake is yellow, and all I have in the house are red ones."

You see, the subtle point of the thing is that the man considers these things *petty*—that is, unless he is the one about whom the fuss is being made. You will never really appreciate a woman unless you have seen her at the end of a day of moving into a new flat, the furniture in disarray, the children bedded in makeshift bunks, quietly putting up the nicely ironed curtains. The mere male dwindles in stature as the woman unobtrusively proves that the dignity of the human soul transcends time and circumstance. It is no wonder that God entrusted His Divine Son as a gentle Babe to the warm, confident love of a valiant woman.

A fellow and girl have to be equipped with a great deal more than mutual infatuation if they hope to survive the difficulties of marriage. During the course of married life I have picked up a working set of principles that help to make for compatibility between the sexes.

To begin with, it is not an easy thing for a man and woman to get along together. I stress this point especially for young lovers who have not yet had a real spat. If there comes a time or occasion when you would be delighted to subject your mate to some form of mayhem, do not consider yourself peculiar. Resist the urge to inflict injury, by all means, but do not for a moment conclude that your marriage is shattered or that love has fled. Saint Paul said that marriage is a great mystery. Every husband and wife has learned that it is a mystery for which there is no solution except love.

The family relationship is a dynamic one. By that I mean that it is a living, moving, maturing relationship. It is not static. It is not the relation between a nut and a bolt, or between a set of gears. The man and woman must become one flesh. Their two lives must fuse together and yet remain vital. The man is not consumed by the woman nor is she consumed by the man. They must be joined together without any loss of personality. In fact, when a marriage is successful, the personalities of both husband and wife become more mature, more vital. The man becomes more manly, and the woman becomes more feminine.

To make this possible, the two sexes must not only attract one another, but they must also repel one another. This may sound like a contradiction, but it can easily be demonstrated. It is normal, for example, for a man to be attracted to a woman, but it is equally normal for him to be repelled by femininity. No normal man would want to live in a beribboned and scented boudoir. On the other hand, it is normal for a woman to love a man; it is equally normal for her to be repelled by masculinity. No normal woman would like the loud talk, rough comradeship and bare decoration of a barracks or clubroom. The point to be stressed is that a man may love a woman, but he hates to be womanly. A woman may love a man, but she has no desire to be manly.

The love, then, that should exist between husband and wife can be expected to have the qualities of reverence and respect. In other words, when a husband loves his wife, he must love her because she is a woman and love her as a woman should be loved. He cannot love her as a pal and treat her like one of his football chums. The wife must love her husband because he is a man, and love him as a man should be loved. She must not treat him like a child or regard him as a sorority sister.

In this way, we respect the mystery of marriage. The man will never thoroughly understand the woman and usually admits it. The woman will never thoroughly understand the man, but will seldom admit it. Because of this mystery, the love of a man for a woman has a special character that makes it different from the love of a woman for a man. The nearest we can come to defining this difference is to say that the love of the man must be *considerate*, and the love of the woman must be *acquiescent*.

I could take a few cases from my own experience to show you what I mean by consideration and acquiescence. Suppose I were to work late at the office. As I approach the house after getting off the bus, I try to phrase my excuse in advance so as to placate my wife's very understandable ire at having "spoiled" her dinner. In my mind, the whole excuse boils down to the fact that I just *had* to work late. That's all there is to it! I had to work late. So, when I open the door and behold the frown, I say, "I'm awfully sorry, dear, for being late, but I just *had to* work late!" The thunder cloud is not so easily dispelled. But, after all, I *did have to* work late, didn't I?

Before abstracting any lesson from this, let's consider the opposite situation, when I get home on time and my wife doesn't have the supper ready. Dorothy immediately goes into a lengthy and elaborate explanation: "You see, dear, Mrs. O'Connor called me over to meet Abigail Updyke, who is engaged to Mrs. O'Connor's son. You can imagine my surprise when I discovered that Abigail went to school with Daphne Hothouse. You *know* Daphne, she was at our wedding—wore a silk taffeta skirt with a belt in the back—Well, you see, Mrs. O'Connor was awfully anxious to make Abigail feel at ease and she was delighted to discover that I have something in common with her— So, you see, one thing led to another. . . ."

This explanation cannot be stemmed. It continues through supper and beyond. Finally, just before going to sleep, my wife breaks into tears, "You simply won't forgive me for not having your dinner ready, will you?" Of course, I have already repeated at fifteen minute intervals for the past four hours, "That's perfectly all right, dear, don't let it bother you one little bit." Naturally, near the end, my words of forgiveness had a slight note of "For *Heaven's sake*, forget it, will ya?"

I don't intend to pass out a formula for handling such

situations as these. My intention is only to demonstrate what I mean by consideration and acquiescence. Please notice that the husband's crisp and precise explanation would have been quickly accepted by another man and the wife's lengthy and elaborate excuse would have met the approval of another woman. In the second case (where the wife makes the excuse), the husband's consideration for the feminine nature of the wife could make the whole thing come off very neatly. He should come to expect lengthy excuses (for that's a woman's way). If, for example, he showed a *certain amount of enthusiasm* for his wife's story (which she is elaborating to take his attention away from her negligence), the first thing you know is that the entire attention would be centered on the story, and the late supper would be forgotten.

In the first case, if the wife were to acquiesce to the masculine habit of crisp explanations, and *accept it as a precise statement of fact,* everything would be fine. She need merely say, "Of course, dear, you had to work late, that can't be helped."

Consideration is an active, aggressive virtue. Acquiescence is a passive, docile virtue. The husband has to summon up his enthusiasm for his wife's lengthy story. The wife has to quiet and pacify her anger at his being late, and also squelch her curiosity for details.

Another example that illustrates consideration and acquiescence is the formality of a man's opening a door for a lady. Picture a couple, arm-in-arm, approaching a closed door. For the entire formality to come off gracefully, the girl must *step back* and the fellow must *step forward.* If the fellow fails to step forward the girl feels that she has been ill treated. If, on the other hand, the

girl fails to step back, the man must either roughly push
her aside or else follow her shamefacedly through the
doorway. The same kind of consideration and acquiescence are necessary in every intersexual act.

Why should this be so? Human experience throughout
the ages prescribes that in every joint enterprise of men
and women, the man must lead. It would be foolish to
defend this male leadership here; the defensive position
belongs to those who doubt it, or who would try to produce a plausible alternative. As individuals, men and
women have been endowed by God with an equality in
dignity and potential. They do not, however, have the
same function to fill in society. It is merely in this role,
when their functions are wed to conceive a joint enterprise, that the leadership falls to the man. It is only
when men exploit their leadership by active brutality
or passive weakness that women refuse to accept the
supporting role. Today is just such an era of brutality
and weakness. Consequently, there has been a concerted
endeavor on the part of women to throw off a yoke that
robs them of their dignity. If it is true (and history
proves it so) that a woman gains full stature and great
dignity beside a virtuous and virile husband, it is equally
true that a weak man will have a debilitating effect upon
his wife.

Human nature does not change, however. If it is true
that the men of our generation exhibit a gross brutality
in their war and a shameful weakness in their peace,
failure on the part of women to acquiesce will do nothing more than aggravate the situation. The wife who
refuses to accept the dignity of a supporting role forces
her husband to be either brutal or weak. There is no
alternative to mutual harmony, and the requirement

will always be that the man be eternally considerate of the sensitive nature of the woman and the woman acquiesce to the active aggressiveness of her husband. Sacrifice and great charity are needed in either case.

I suppose any fellow or girl who ever paused to consider the privilege of being married and of accepting its responsibilities has asked himself if he were worthy or adequate. At one time I thought that I was a bad risk. Suddenly my marrying Dot seemed like a dirty trick on her. My health was not too good. I had a chronic ailment as the result of an early football injury. I'm no genius, especially at making money. Along with that, I have certain principles that I wouldn't violate for any pay-check, a resolve that had made me disliked by more than one boss.

Without being morbid, just being honest with myself, I had to admit I was a bad marital risk. Yet I marshalled the courage to take the plunge, and I have weathered other periods of misgivings which persist to the present day. The key to the riddle is my faith.

Any parent who has ever taken his new baby in his arms and looked at it has had an experience that should have touched his head as well as his heart. No one could believe for a moment, unless he were a presumptuous fool, that this unbelievably wonderful creature, so perfect and brand new, could be an effect of which he and his wife were the sole and simple cause. Could either of you, who hardly know how to care for this creature, who fumble with many thumbs to sustain it, be so foolish as to suppose this child is wholly *yours?* The bare minimum of humility demands a "No!"

This moment can be priceless. It is easy to see a great mystery here. There is a special grace from God that comes with the first visible fruit of matrimony. You suddenly see yourselves as participators in a tremendous drama in which the elements are real and the stake is life. Your part is a great privilege, but a simple task. God has fashioned a body and soul. You had a part in it, but how little a part, considering this wonderful, tangible, vital infant. With this there should come an awful awareness of the presence of God. This God, Who can in His perfection transcend all things, deigns to become an intimate of our home. His presence here is warm with life. Our babies grow mysteriously; we merely feed and wash them. Then come words and ideas. A new will exerts itself against the bars of the crib. A new consciousness watches the visitor and recognizes the parent. A new personality makes its mark on the high-chair and eventually on the world.

You see yourself working along with God. He has enlisted your aid, not you His. He has made you His agent. It is His plan, His scheme of things, His harvest. You are in attendance, removing the obstacles to His workings. It is in the light of this that the idea of being a bad risk is defeated.

For who *is* a good risk? In what way does a million dollars, bountiful health, or human genius guarantee a successful marriage? Are these safeguards against conflicting wills, sickness or poverty? Not at all! The things that make for happy marriages, as anyone who is happily married can testify, are intangible things that moths do not consume nor thieves abscond with. In fact, it is money and the power it gives, it is human genius with its ugly pride, and it is the constant concern about opinions and possessions, to which divorcees attribute their failure.

Trust in God not only is a guarantee of our needs, as Christ promised it would be, but it also disposes our minds and wills to bear with the difficulties of conflicting wills. God's spiritual gifts of mutual charity and trust are far more precious and indispensable than His bounty in providing bread.

Knowing this, I told my wife right at the beginning that there was only one reason why she should trust me in spite of my obvious failings. That reason was that I trusted God. The strength of our family would not depend upon Daddy's right arm, his foresight, his intrepid character, but rather upon the infinite mercy of God, Who is more concerned for our good than we are, and far more capable of providing for it. There are three providers in our house, Christ and His two agents, my wife and I.

The faithfulness of partners in marriage is a thing seldom discussed. Those who are unfaithful usually try to keep their infidelity a secret, and those who are not, consider infidelity as something "nice people don't do." This secretive attitude might be appropriate were it not for the fact that infidelity is no longer a rare and isolated event, but rather a social epidemic. Conversations in shops, clubrooms, and offices would be enough to indicate its prevalence, but in addition we have the infidelity of pre-marital sex relations, and the infidelity of tandem marriages.

To regard unfaithfulness as the isolated and strictly personal affair of the parties concerned is to overlook the entire significance of human contract. The bond which unites men harmoniously in society is trust in a common God, and trust in one another. All human relations depend for their proper resolution on an exchange of trust and confidence. At the root of each social contract, whether between co-partners in business or between nations, lies the most sacred, most selfless, and most intimate of all contracts—marriage. Nowhere, apart from the strict profession of religious life, do you find a greater relinquishing of human privilege for the sake of a common goal than in marriage.

The ultimate infidelity, divorce, strikes a murderous blow at the innocent children who cannot but be left with a wound that grows fetid with mistrust and cynicism. As the children grow, they carry a wariness into their relations with others. The divorce society shies away from all commitments and violates every contract. When this paranoia becomes political you have something like Soviet Russia and Nazi Germany—mistrust and persecution manias hover like ghosts over the conference table, and wars are waged in the name of imaginary injustices.

From each family flows a tiny spring that empties into the moral reservoir of society. Here at its source the waters are either purified or polluted. When the pollution has reached the reservoir the moral health of every social institution is jeopardized.

Standing watch over this entire process of human intercourse is the virtue of chastity. This picture of guardianship would be ludicrous were we to portray chastity in the role assigned her by the prude or the libertine. It is to the advantage of those who reap personal or corporate profit from moral degeneracy to reduce chastity to the level of a cartoonist's old maid whose only claim to fame is a record of "no hits, no runs, no errors." If we look at the thing boldly, however, and realize that the fate of nations depends upon the inviolability of contracts, and that the marriage contract is the keystone in the contractual arch, and that chastity is the guardian of the marital act, then we must conceive of a virtue—of an adequacy—that demands the heroic.

Chastity fills this role and fills it well. It is in the pure splendor of new love that chastity takes root in marriage, when the young lovers regard their union as inviolate. Their ardor would abhor nothing as much as infidelity. This vital tree is cultivated through sickness, trials and failures, and bears fruit and casts seeds as their children are betrothed and marry. There is no greater tribute of man to man than this concentration of love on one person undeterred. Infidelity is the love-tragedy, the ultimate betrayal of every human confidence.

The alarming thing about infidelity is its ability to grow without studied malice. Those who bertay their wives or husbands usually do not violate their vow in hatred, but in despair. Their passions refuse to be subservient to their love. Consequently, the enemy to be sought out and destroyed is not infidelity or divorce, but the virus which breaks down resistance. The name of the virus is immodesty.

When we concentrate upon immodesty our inquiry covers a broader social field. The provocations to lust are not limited to those areas where lust can be satisfied. The unhappy fact is that very chaste women frequently dress as though they were advertisements for infidelity. Thus the theatre and movies, the advertisements and novels, the styles and postures, spread their propaganda for lust into every home, and those who feel the least vulnerable may be the first to become infected.

The most striking evidence for this is the impossibility of finding today a living symbol for the chaste spouse, the valiant woman; yet within a hundred yards of wherever you may be, you can find in print or in the flesh a symbol of female prostitution. It was just such a lack of a dignified symbol that recently led a young Jewish psychologist to the discovery of the Blessed Virgin Mary.

In her, he saw woman glorified, fruitful, valiant and inviolate. In her, he saw a modesty that was not a posture, but an exterior radiance that clothed her dynamic vitality. Summed up in all the veneration extended to Mary throughout the ages, he saw the challenge to today's glorification of the street-walker. He concluded, as I have concluded, that the salvation of human fidelity and the sacredness of contracts ultimately depend upon the veneration of womanhood glorified. Fortunately for us, Christ has given us not merely a symbol but a mother of flesh and blood who stands through time and eternity as the prototype of humanity redeemed, invulnerable to sin, triumphant over temptation, free from treachery.

George Bernard Shaw once said that if a man lived three hundred years he would know everything. G. K. Chesterton answered, "Yes, and if Shaw lived three hundred years, he would be a Catholic." The point Shaw had in mind when he made the crack was that history tends to repeat itself. Mankind is always sitting in the pasture of history, rechewing its own cud. In any three-hundred-year period all theories and revolutions prove themselves either true or untrue, either sane or insane. What Chesterton had in mind was that any man who saw his own life-span within a perspective of three hundred years would see the logic of Christianity and the need of a Church to perpetuate that logic through history.

Q

To understand marriage we must also regard it from a perspective that embraces a number of generations, otherwise we do not see it *wholly*. Matrimony is a love affair, but it is a love affair in which many more than two people take part. Two is company, but it takes at least three to make a family.

Suppose, for instance, that we look at marriage according to the current mores; what do we see? We see two people in love. They are young and at the height of their idealism and vigor. They marry. The first few months are preoccupied with mutual adoration. Reasonably and observably this can't go on forever. When the fever-heat of the honeymoon has cooled, what is left? They usually try to bank the fire and, while reducing its intensity, attempt to extend its quiet warmth throughout the years. As time goes on, and the lovers grow in age, their attempts at maintaining their love become frantic and all-absorbing. In their narrow scheme of things the climax has passed and all that is left is a prolonged and inevitable anti-climax. They proceed from youth to old age, and finally to the grave. Their love story is more tragic than that of Romeo and Juliet. It is suicidal, but a suicide extended over many dull years, rather than over a few dramatic moments.

But contrasted with this concept of marriage, let's try to see it in the perspective of generations. Two people meet, each of them an heir to a valuable heritage. They bring to the altar an inheritance of culture, of wisdom and of faith. Their ancestors suffered, died, endured sea voyages, imprisonment, preserving this treasure which the two lovers offer one another when they plight their troth. In their marital embrace they generate the seed of a new generation who will take these historic

gifts and weave them together in a new pattern—a new
way of life. The process of events is no longer tragic,
because as the lovers grow old they see their early vigor
transplanted in their children. The children become
adept at using the cherished culture, wisdom and faith.
This glorious tradition blossoms anew within the family.
The parents are unaware of their declining years and
passing youth because they are too engrossed, cultivat-
ing a new and more wonderful life in their children.

Without this conception of marriage as a vehicle for
extending a life of culture, wisdom and faith throughout
the years, the entire adventure and the very reason for
marriage is lost. Without it marriage is a flash in the pan,
a glorious sky-rocket that drops in a moment, charred
and inert. We cannot, however, maintain this conception
of marriage unless we truly cherish the culture, wisdom
and faith to which we are heirs. If *life* for us means no
more than the thing that began at our birth and ends
with our death, then we, in truth, have no troth to plight.
We are asking our beloved to wed tomorrow's cadaver,
to share a requiem, to share our grave.

The Christian home is a shrine that glorifies a living
culture, wisdom and faith. It is not a museum for the
accumulation of outmoded gestures, relics of the past,
but a place of new birth. In the children the faith comes
to life, taking on new forms, developing unique social
patterns.

All the moralizing against birth control is almost
always in vain unless this vital conception of marriage
is retained. Who would have children if the end of childhood were nothing but a dull wait for death? Who would
want children if he had no treasure to offer them? Who
would give life unless life had an eternal significance,

dating back to Genesis and extending forward to eternal union with God?

In the modern scheme of things the child too often comes as an obstacle to the parents' wallowing in their own childish and selfish indulgences; whereas in the Christian scheme of things the child becomes the focus of family concern, the new messenger, the new apostle, to carry the flame through another generation.

Realizing this, Dorothy and I are trying to revive the cultural patterns of the past and adapt them to the new generation in which Ann and Marie, Paul and Michael, Elizabeth, Peter and Clare, will live. We want them to know and appreciate the Christian thing as it was appreciated in ages past, as it is understood today by the Catholic natives of Hong Kong, of Czechoslovakia, of Italy. During the weeks before Christmas our Advent wreath is hung and its candles lighted, while the sole absorption of many neighbors is with Christmas shopping. Christ comes into our house on Christmas Day and the Infant remains with us through the Epiphany. The children learn of the exchange of gifts, the constant beneficence of God. Later we go through Lent. Michael learns a new significance for the bumped head and the scraped shin-bone as he vaguely perceives the positive value of suffering. Easter is a glorious reward for the endurance of fasts and penances, consonant with the children's age and capacity.

The significance centers not in pious gestures, but the children are taught the Christ-life lived. Justice and charity in their dealings with playmates. The ingenious use of poverty in their little arts, such as those exemplified in the carpenter shop at Nazareth.

Slowly they will perceive the vast Christian mission

and their part in it, the splendid adventure of restoring to Christ a world that has strayed. Their pettiness will be replaced by a docility to greatness. They will become alarmed at the vacuity of selfishness and let that vacuum be filled with divine purposefulness.

Children mean just that to us. We do not pray and work so that everything will *go* well. Our concern is that everything will *grow* well. Will we try to become better-off for the sake of the children? No! We will try to become better for the sake of the children, because by becoming better we will become closer to God Who is the source of all good, material and spiritual, and because we have learned that the desire to become better-off is just as likely to exclude children as to include them.

The last few paragraphs may be a little top-heavy with the idea of placing traditional burdens on young shoulders. We haven't forgotten that each child has a life of its own to be led. A child never goes according to the book. Each one is unique, and the formula for each one's happiness differs in details from that of the other.

Persons who have no children usually possess dogmatic principles for raising them. It is sheer poetry to envisage children as either saints or devils. Experience proves that each child is a unique combination of conflicting elements. The parent must strive gently to resolve those conflicts, always respecting the delicate instrument with which he works. When a child does something against the wishes of the parent his motive may be either weakness, love, malice, ignorance, fear or imitation. For example, Mike constantly strays out of the neighborhood. We have had to put the police on his tail at various times. Should this crime be treated as malicious disobedience? No! Mike has a memory that doesn't retain a thing. He proceeds from one wonderful experience to the other. Even on the way to the wood-shed his anticipation is forgotten in the delight of watching a passing butterfly! Virtue must be made adventurous for Mike or he's not interested.

Marie is sent to the corner store. She returns an hour later with some strange tale and no groceries. Marie is timid and she just waits until the proprietor finds her down below the counter. Paul talks back to his Grandma simply in imitation of the sport he has with the neighbors' teen-age boys. Here and there there is malice, unbalanced nature, original sin forcing its way through. Each of the motives must be recognized. Malice is punished. Imitation is channeled. Ignorance is instructed. Fear is dispelled. Weakness is strengthened. Never is the will bent too far, but only slowly and carefully, in keeping with its nature.

Influence in the home is by no means one-sided. If the family dynamic is working properly while the children are being counseled by the parents as to the ways of adulthood, the parents are being reminded by the youngsters of the virtues of childhood. Any parent who is honest with himself has his tongue in his cheek whenever he says, "I don't know why it is that Junior persists in doing the things I tell him not to do!" At such a time he cannot but think of his own disobedience and perversity in relation to God. Why do we, the parents, persist in our disobedience to God?

What adult, when talking to a youngster, does not envy his guilelessness and sincerity? His upturned face so open and sincere? Often I have brought worries home only to have them dispelled by the gaiety of the children. Their happy innocence gives us a nostalgia for the innocence of the sons of God. "Unless you become like little children," Christ said, "you will not enter into the Kingdom of Heaven." How fortunate to have the evidences of childhood all around us to pin-prick our sophistications and remind us of our helplessness before God.

Adulthood can become an awfully grim and desperate state unless it is tempered by the sanity of childhood. Yet the homes today are few and far between in which you can find that elusive ingredient. The vogue now is to tolerate the child within an adult milieu. Mother and father keep their world autonomous, limiting the children to play-pens. The children are bribed with toys to keep their distance. The tribulations of the child are treated as so many "cases" with the formal competence more becoming to a social worker than a parent.

Fortunately, with a brood as large as ours childhood cannot be relegated to an area. It's all over the place. Lonely children sense this and seek out our home as though it were an oasis. In spite of their electric toys and three-shift tricycles, they would rather spend their time among our youngsters. In the eyes of the children, it is our brood who are privileged because our home is *for* children, not for grownups. In other houses you may find a child, but in our house you can find *childhood*.

One experience we had that has done much to relieve us of fears and worries was that which occurred about four years ago. We were expecting our fourth baby. We were living fairly snugly in a furnished attic in a pleasant neighborhood. Things had become somewhat crowded since the time we had moved there as starry-eyed newly-weds. The landlady didn't like our propensity for propagation. She didn't like the wailing and gnashing of teethings, and she also felt that large families reduced the value of real estate; this, in spite of the fact that we had painted and decorated the exterior and interior of the house. She had asked us to leave.

We had gone about on Sunday afternoons, scouting the area for vacant flats. If there had been some way by which we could have boiled down our three children into one dog, we might have made the grade with some landlords.

This had not bothered us too much until my wife became pregnant. The attendant increased sensitiveness made her more vulnerable to the scathing remarks of the landlady. We were also learning that having a large family so close together incurred the same social stigma as chronic drunkenness or dope-peddling. Our neighbors and relatives compounded a hypocritical concern for our plight with an equally obvious unwillingness to assist us in any way. Our spirits were at a low ebb.

At that time I was working as a shipping clerk in a warehouse. We were very busy and overworked. My chronic ailment had become worse. In addition to that, I had been giving all my leisure hours to the preparations for the yet unborn magazine *Integrity*.

One evening a friend of mine dropped in to mind the children while Dot and I went to see the doctor. He had unpleasant news for us. "It is impossible," he told us, "at this late date to make a hospital appointment for your wife." The hospitals were overcrowded and beds were scarce. The second piece of news was that I had to take a month in bed, or else.

Well, that was the picture when we went home that night. Here were all the circumstances that trembling newly-weds foresee with horror. Sickness, eviction and childbirth, and no money in the bank. The way the thing worked out has only re-confirmed our trust in God and taught us something about the way He acts.

We prayed and asked the prayers of others. We encouraged one another and went ahead with our plans. To my great surprise the company paid my salary for the month of absence. I felt no compunction in accepting it because I had spared no effort in their behalf during the preceding two years. The rest left me free to concentrate on the magazine plans, undisturbed by the urgency that I had felt before. My wife was shunted to another, less expensive doctor, who found her a bed in a truly Christian hospital, and her lying-in period was the happiest she had known.

Shortly after my recovery, I came to New York where we were planning to publish the magazine. My associates and I made a novena of prayers, and I placed an advertisement in the newspaper reading, "Undesirable tenant wishes to rent apartment. Have four children and will probably have more." There was one answer. A small house, badly in need of repairs, was available on the outskirts of the city. I plastered up the sagging ceilings, repaired the furnace, and we all moved in.

In retrospect it is obvious that what we had at first considered to be great troubles were actually the stepping-stones to great treasures. When we were at what appeared to be the depth of our miseries we were in fact on the threshold of a new adventure. The poets have made much of this universal experience, phrasing it in such ways as "the darkest hour is just before the dawn."

The Christian can see a more mysterious element and abstract a more profound conclusion.

God desires our faith, or complete trust in Him. He permits troubles and fears to arise so as to strengthen our faith, much as a football coach will drill his squad vigorously so that their strength will grow. Every ill to which the human being is prone exists singly for the purpose of our placing our trust in God. We do this by bearing with the suffering, but always with the realization that we will at last be triumphant.

If we reject the trial through timidity, we inevitably reject the triumph, and fail to gain the reward. A man who resorts to dishonesty in order to swing a deal because he fears that honesty will gain him nothing, by so doing erects an obstacle between himself and God's providence. A new baby has often been the occasion for a husband's getting a promotion and a wife's regaining her health. Yet most people deny themselves children on the erroneous presumption that a new baby inevitably means unhappiness. In their denial of the sacrifice they turn away from God's bounty. God's concern for them, His desire for their happiness, is continuous and generous, but they through timidity refuse to grasp the cross which will release the treasure.

The enemies of Christianity have always used whatever weapons might be lying around, without regard for truth or fair play. The communist weapon is slander. They do not condemn a Christian belief for what it is but try to prove it is something else, less grand, less desirable. Ever since the death of Christ there has been a campaign on foot to deform His simple teachings. One of the most subtle of these lies is the one that makes a trust in God's providence *appear to be* an alibi for sloth and irresponsibility. It is true that a religious man is not money-hungry, nor does he want to get the best of his neighbor in a deal, but it is not true that a trust in God makes him less diligent.

The married man today must trust in God, and that implies much more work and greater ingenuity than he would need if he were single, or without faith. Society makes little, if any, provision for the responsibilities of parenthood. The prices of children's clothing, rents, doctors' bills and natal care are all in the luxury bracket. Yet there is no corresponding increase in his income. He must shoulder all the extra burdens that go with sustaining unproductive children, and rather than receiving help he is considered foolish, ostracized from many areas of the city, charged exorbitant sums for children's clothing, excluded from associations he can no longer afford to belong to; and frequently he must work for longer hours at a lower rate of pay.

All this requires hard work and ingenuity. The father of a normal-sized family must learn to take care of as many of his own needs as possible. He can't afford to be without a set of simple tools and the knowledge of how to use them. He must be able to make minor electrical, carpentry, plumbing and mechanical repairs. The wife, in turn, must also, in spite of her additional burdens, acquire skills that will lessen the need for calling in experts.

My wife has saved many dollars of doctors' bills by learning to diagnose and treat minor ailments. We have learned the proper procedure in first aid and medical treatments for the innumerable germs and accidents that invade a family. Not long ago, by a simple trip to the distributor's and fifteen minutes with a screw-driver,

I saved $9.50 on a repair bill for my refrigerator. Things have to be really bad before we must resort to doctors' fees and the bills of repair men.

Beyond this there is the need to keep our children entertained as well, and with far less money than that expended by our less productive neighbors. We must teach them games and build them toys. The toys must be beyond comparison with the store-gotten fantasies showered on the pampered kid next door. We must instill in our children a sense of leadership, so that they will not grow timid under the persecution that nice people dish out to what they so hypocritically term "the underprivileged."

Trust in God implies a mighty diligence and an adventurous ingenuity. Please notice that under the time-honored system of Christian marriage, husbandry and house-wifery are not the moronic vocations that the careerist deceitfully claims they are. A father who places *life* first, who not only accepts children but really provides for them, is likely to make more decisions in a day than a business executive makes in a month. His life is intensely interesting. There is no time for boredom. He must be a philosopher, a craftsman, a politician, a doctor, a psychologist, an administrator and a poet. His wife must be a nurse, a teacher, an artist, a hostess, and a director of souls. The society of the future is made under the eyes and hands of the mother and father, for after the child leaves the home the fate of society and his role in it has already been decided.

It is no surprise that today's family has come in for such a beating once you realize that the family spirit is just the opposite to cut-throat competition. No one expects that one of a gang of robbers holding up a bank will stop to pick up a lady's handkerchief or help an old lady across the street with her bundles. For the same reason you can't expect the family spirit to survive in a society where everyone is concerned with *self*-expression, *self*-aggrandizement, and even the religious people solely concerned with *self*-improvement. This is especially true when the idea of self-improvement is divorced from the traditionally Christian notion that the way to self-improvement is self-sacrifice.

Christ told us we must love God and love our neighbor. He did not need to tell us to love ourselves or further our own ambitions. If we really want to be perfect and perfectly happy, we gain this state by seeking the happiness of others and not bothering too much about ourselves.

I have already indicated that this modern self-centeredness makes a unity between the husband and wife thoroughly impossible. The modern man and woman lack the generosity for sacrifice that is required before two bodies and two souls can work in harmony. It is precisely this self-centeredness that the Sacrament of Christian Matrimony was designed by God to erase.

Christian Matrimony provides a God-given grace that sublimates our natures, so that the man and wife are enabled to overcome their human selfishness and to become docile to the daily task that lies before them. This grace not only tends to unite man and wife, but it also unites family with family. This is a fact that my wife and I discovered only after many preliminary mistakes.

You see, we were a pair of starry-eyed idealists when we walked away from the matrimonial altar, hand-in-hand. I'm not sorry about that. If there is one time when the heart should be filled with daring plans and great adventure, it should be on the day of marriage. Because we were idealists, we knew the scorn which the modern world has for ideals. It isn't the man who can hold an ideal that is admired today, but the man who can swing a deal. Our contemporaries are not interested in prophets but in profits.

Even before we were married the persons were few and far between who truly *encouraged* us in our hopes. Everyone and his brother, it seems, feels obligated to warn the prospective bride and bridegroom of the precautions that must be taken against disaster, even the disaster of having children. Advice for the engaged has the grim quality of modern bookkeeping that fastens its eyes not on success but upon bankruptcy and re-sale. After being subject for so long to such wet-blanket counsels, we decided to keep our ideals to ourselves. We were not marrying on speculation, we were playing for keeps. If no one believed this, then we would keep it as our own secret.

As we furnished our home and had our first children, and developed family customs, we kept pretty much to ourselves. We were friendly with our neighbors and relatives, but never intimate. We did not wish to have our ideals challenged. We wanted a Christian family life without having to defend our position at every step.

The time came, however, when we saw that things cannot be handled quite so neatly. An ideal is not a thing that is meant to be hung as an immaculate sword above the fireplace, but a thing to become bloodstained and muddy in battle. The occasion for this lesson was the arrival of our third baby.

At that time we had neither a telephone nor a car (today we have a telephone). As is inevitable, the first

pangs of childbirth came at the cold, unholy hour of
4:00 A.M. I had to fumble into my clothes, run across the
street to a neighbor, wake him and beg the use of his
phone. I received no response to my calls for a taxi, and
had to go to another neighbor for the use of his car.
Much to my delight and humiliation, the same neighbors whom I had tried to keep out of my affairs so assid-
uously were extremely generous when I asked them to
help me with my affairs. If I had wished to do so, I could
have taken a vacation at that time and left the care of
the two children to these friendly women. I did not do
this, but I did gain a far more valuable service from them
because I learned in an unforgettable way that the
family cannot and should not, no matter what its ideals
may be, exist for itself, but that it must be part of a community of families.

The fact that these people, in times of emergency,
leaped happily to the aid of a family in need, proved to
me that if this same neighborliness were revived as a
continuous social attitude, each individual family would
have a far greater chance of survival, as well as an opportunity to grow normally.

Having our ideals challenged did us no harm. Most
of our neighbors had accepted in varying degrees the
sterile and fatal prescription for marriage dispensed by
the popular magazines and upheld by popular opinion.
They did not regard children as a blessing but as a
burden. The women were more intent upon retaining the
appearance of youth than gaining the dignity of dedicated motherhood. The husbands were more concerned
about making more money, than passing on to their
children a spiritual bank account that can never be over-
drawn. Making friends with such people meant many

an argument, and a certain weariness at defending our principles. But, as I say, it was worth it. We were forced by such intimate contact to re-examine our stand. If we were right, we became more convinced. Where we had become spiritual snobs, we were forced to admit it. Many of the people who would not accept our high ideals practised a charity in their lives far greater than ours. Some who practised birth control were more patient with the children they had than we were with ours.

We learned, above all, that despite any difference of religious views or practical policies, God intended that we should *need* one another. We learned that our family was only a small part of a larger and greater family. We became aware in a very practical way of the implication of that magnificent Christian teaching called the Mystical Body of Christ: that all men are part one of the other, and the head of that Body is Christ.

This was not all we learned. The more we sought to live in charity with our neighbors, the more we observed the universal hunger that people have for the spiritual food the Church dispenses. Sometimes, for example, in the course of an evening's conversation, we would mention a Christian truth that we had come to look upon as commonplace. Our guests would be amazed and ask us to repeat it. They would carry it away as a treasure, and before long they would have made it so important a part of their lives that we would be ashamed at having let it become commonplace.

God makes use of the community as an instrument of His providence. No family has everything it needs all the time. Few families have everything they need at any time. Yet if many families were to add up their needs and possessions in a collective pool, perhaps all of them would be able to extract all that they needed at a given time. I can hear harsh words of "communism" in the background, but that is utter nonsense. Wherever people have lived together in harmony since the beginning of time there has always been a spirit of mutual co-operation. It is thoroughly perverse for any family to be forced to conclude that it is completely dependent upon its own efforts. Yet this is the spirit of today. So afraid are we to depend upon our neighbors in time of need that we timidly hoard every penny against such a day. Private property is a good thing and so is thrift, but if the emphasis on them is so great that each family becomes an independent kingdom, then society will destroy itself.

At the present time I am engaged in building a group of houses in company with fourteen other families. We have been at it but a short time, yet long enough to see the tremendous benefits of neighborly co-operation. First of all, hardly any of us would have considered the possibility of owning our own homes, for, since we have large families and average incomes, we could not possibly afford it. It is yet to be proved that we can do it or afford to do it in a group, but we are working as though it were possible. This working together has given us new assurance and moral courage. We have helped each other in various ways and will grow in knowledge of community co-operation. Already men have learned skills and wives have re-confirmed one another's faith in Christian living. Each family knows that if it suffers it will not suffer alone, and if it prospers the others will rejoice. We are not competing against one another, but seeking a common goal as a complementary company of neighbors.

R

The alternative to this is for each family to go ahead, seeking its own, letting the Devil take the hindmost. Yet every family that breaks up, or becomes dependent upon the state for support, threatens the entire society of families. New laws are invoked to meet the breakdown of the family, and these laws limit the liberty of other families as well as condoning the weakness. The fact that most families can no longer own property has caused us to lose a respect for property. This, in turn, causes us to relax our vigilance against the development of a government policy which will eventually make ownership completely impossible. The municipal apartment dwellings are an insult to a free people: concrete birdhouses for government wards so small that there is no room for children. We can neither rant nor fume against this unless we seek the only alternative: free co-operation of families to build houses in spread-out areas, where there will be room for children, shops, vegetable gardens and livestock.

It is very sad that engaged couples and newly-weds when they are young and vigorous cannot be persuaded to join forces with others and do things in a community way. When the third and fourth child come along it is hard then to face the obvious fact that our urban society does not *want* normal families. They suddenly realize that they must rely on their own efforts at a time when their cares and burdens are greatest.

Thank Heaven, more and more men are buying tools and meeting at planning sessions. More and more wives are sewing together, shopping together, and minding each other's babies. There is some residual Christian liberty and American independence left, so that a welfare state and a communist state will not evolve without our putting up a good fight. Families are coming together, yours and mine, and discovering this splendid thing—a community

Not long ago my wife and I had a few moments of peace together. I had arrived home from the office after a day of tiring conferences, capped by the usual hour on the subway. The seven children were having their supper and my wife's hectic day was at its climax. Ann had been told in school that she needed glasses. Marie had pictures to show me which she had painted in kindergarten. Paul was in line for a spanking for having resisted a neighbor's attempts to remove him from the rear bumper of his car. Michael had a cold. Elizabeth had fallen downstairs. Peter's new tooth had blossomed beautifully in the middle of his grin. Clare too had a cold.

We organized the rambunctious crew through their supper, washed them up, packaged them in their pyjamas and lined them up for prayers. Paul was able to get through the "Hail Mary" without any help. Michael characteristically thanked God and asked God for "food." Elizabeth made the others giggle when she said "blessed is the soup" instead of "blessed is the fruit."

Prayers having been finished, we tucked them in bed. Everything had been tended to except listening to Ann's "reading." God bless you's were exchanged and Dot and I sat down at the kitchen table to eat our cooled-off dinner. Surprisingly enough, the children went immediately to sleep. We became suddenly aware of the ticking of the kitchen clock—things were as quiet as that!

Suddenly a feeling of great peace descended upon us. We lingered over a second cup of tea and began to reminisce. Nine years of married life were behind us. We talked about our various experiences together. I asked Dot which of these experiences struck her as being the happiest. We both knitted our brows and tried to remember. After a while Dot said, "You know, I don't think I was ever more happy with you than I am right at this moment." I had to admit with some surprise that I felt the same way!

Ours, we think, is a successful marriage. How do we account for success when all the trials and troubles we go through are the very things that other people avoid as pitfalls? I suppose that at the root of the happiness is a mystery. Through a process of elimination, we always arrive at the conclusion that it is nothing but God's helping grace. We are living a Sacrament. All the other things that seem to explain our peace in the midst of trouble are more an effect than a cause. Certainly a husband's love matures as he sees his wife constantly attentive to the endless demands of the children, rising in a cold bedroom to early-morning emergencies. His love is no longer a fairy-thing, floating in the mirages of courtship. This is a woman with courage and a capacity for sacrifice. She is no stoic, no creature of iron will and vigorous constitution. She is a woman sensitive to pain, yet beyond pain when someone else needs attention. I have not the slightest doubt that come hell or high water, Dot will be right beside me, doing a masterful job. She may weep, but she will work through her tears and she will smile when a smile is needed.

There is a strength far beyond our own that mans the helm of our family ship. Each joy and sorrow has a place in the divine scheme of things. Take one iota of trouble away, and the balance would be lost, the happiness less poignant, the peace less complete. This is Christian marriage, a stark, real, practical, full adventure, a thing of days, nights, years and eternity. The price we pay is merely to reiterate the original vow, "I will," saying over and over again, "Yes," to God and "Yes" to each other.

POSTSCRIPT ON POVERTY AND MARRIAGE

ED WILLOCK

SAINT FRANCIS of Assisi would have acted differently had he been married. You can bet on that. After the "I do's" have been uttered and the golden handcuffs dropped smoothly but firmly on the wrists, any call from the spirit must be answered in writing and endorsed with two signatures. Delightful though it may be, and truly a road to sanctity, matrimony is still a wing-clipping ceremony. Whether a spouse wishes to retire to a local bar for a beer, or a local church for a prayer, due regard must be given to the ties that bind.

This is one side of the story, and the side you are most likely to hear repeated. If this were the complete story, we might conclude that, as far as the married are concerned, Saint Francis was just a holy crack-pot, and we may retire to our Beautyrests undisturbed by any qualms of conscience as to the obligation of holy poverty. Things are not quite so simple as that.

Marriage is not, as so many couples suppose, a brace of tickets for front seats in the amphitheatre from which we may watch the religious and the celibates being thrown to the lions. The road to Calvary is just as rough whether we traverse it single file or in couples. It is still a road of sacrifice. Over and above the fact of the difficulties that line the primrose path there is still the business of voluntary poverty, a self-inflicted detachment from the pottage of life, and it is meant for all Christians whether married or not. Saint Francis would have acted differently had he been married, but this does not mean that he would have divorced Lady Poverty. It means that he would have embraced her in a different way. He would have resolved the paradox of voluntary detachment in the midst of necessary attachment, for this is the special problem of the Christian married.

Catholics in ever-increasing numbers are coming to realize that the Faith in our times is being asphyxiated by an insidious gas called the bourgeois spirit. This spirit is the impetus behind the mystical pilgrimage to the shrine of Mammon frequently referred to as "getting ahead." It is the identification of human happiness with the ever-increasing accumulation of stuff. Even the pagans are becoming sick of it. We have been witness in the past twenty years to a revival of the spirit of holy poverty. It has been spread like a crusade by Dorothy Day and the Catholic Workers. This holy poverty is the one round peg that fits the nasty hole of our vacuous concupiscence.

Many married people have heard this story and like it. They find it hard, however, to relate voluntary poverty to the growing demand for goods that goes with raising a family. The rat race of bargain hunting, overtime work, renewal of furniture, paying the rent, procuring dishes and diapers, dresses and drain-pipes . . . this is a crucifixion they would gladly escape. The sigh goes up, "If we could only afford to be poor! How nice it would be not to *need* all these things!" I have talked the whole business over with people so bothered, and I should like to attempt a kind of ground-plan for marital poverty. It will be brief and incomplete, but it should do something more than scratch the surface.

I think the key to the problem is found in a contrast between the poverty of Saint Francis and the poverty of La Trappe. The poverty of Saint Francis was sudden, spontaneous, complete, and uncalculated. The poverty of the Cistercians is quiet, ordered, partial, and calculated. Both forms of poverty are rigorous enough so that no one can accuse me of watering down. In both cases, poverty is a means to the end of holiness. Yet they differ in practice. Why the difference?

Naked poverty must remain the privilege of those who have no temporal institution to maintain. When Francis stripped himself naked before his Bishop, and ran through the forest singing, he stripped only himself, and he ran alone. He had nothing to lose, and his deprivation deprived no one but himself. On the other hand, once an institution is founded, whether it be a monastery or a family, an order must be devised to sustain it and maintain it. Poverty can only be a means to this end. The rule and the order is the whole, of which poverty is a part. If poverty were to be forgotten in either institution, it would be better that the institution collapse. If poverty became primary, then the institution would collapse. A program of complete poverty can only be pursued at the sacrifice of institutions.

The family must be maintained as an institution, so poverty in marriage should be ordered, partial, and calculated. This does not necessarily limit the fervor of those who seek God, it merely limits the sphere in which the fervor is exercised. A father can still give his heart and mind to God and yet continue to administer property. A mother can give herself to God, but it will be manifested mainly in the service of her husband and children. It's pretty obvious that the home cannot be run as though it were a Trappist monastery. We cannot cut the children down to a minimum diet nor get them out of bed at 2:30 A.M. for Matins and Lauds. Singing the office in choir would have its drawbacks. Without getting too much involved in distinctions, let us say that the family is inclined to operate on the active principle rather than the contemplative and would consequently have a discipline unlike that of La Trappe. For the purposes of defining holy poverty for families, I have taken the liberty of dividing the discipline into four categories. Poverty in the family is specific. It is ingenious. It is communal. It is, above all, patient.

Matrimony is specific. "Do you take *this* woman? I take *thee* John. *This* is my wife. *This* is my home. *These* are my jewels." The choice is emphatic and discriminating. Both nature and grace impose upon the married a specific obligation for specific persons. Since the family exists not only to bear but to raise children, then the parent is obliged to produce and to maintain specific things, *the things that the specific persons need*. The fact that matrimony is specific does not mean that love and affection *terminates* in any one creature or is confined to any four walls, for that is idolatry. What it does mean is that marital love is centripetal, generating outward from a specific love affair, a love affair in which Christ Himself is a partner and the first principle.

Holy poverty in marriage, then, is detachment from all things except those *specific* things that are required to maintain *this* family in the frugal comfort that encourages virtue. The revolutionary implications of this definition may not be immediately obvious. If you just think for a moment about all the things that the advertisers say we *all* need, and then think of how many of these things most of us *do not need at all,* then you get a glimmer. Rooms in which small children play *do not need* shiny waxed floors. Every family *does not need* a car. Every child *should not* go to college. Every child *should not* get a new Easter outfit. Every home *should not* have a washing machine. Every child *should not* have his own bedroom. Without exaggeration, a million such statements could be made. One man's meat is another man's poison. One family's needs are another family's rubbish. Holy poverty rids itself of all impedimenta whether in fact or in desire.

Most families that I know who are trying to practise holy poverty have to a great degree solved the problem of luxuries. They haven't any. This happy state is usually achieved by accepting the beggars that God sends whether by way of the door or by way of the womb. Self-denial then becomes a question of denying one legitimate need so as to provide for another. For example . . .

A mother is badly in need of dental work. The car which Father needs at work is about ready to yield up the ghost for lack of a new clutch. It is possible to afford one, but not both. There's the problem. Whatever the decision, self-denial is involved. If Daddy gets his clutch, he feels like a heel. If Mother has her teeth fixed, she worries about Daddy all day long. Saint John of the Cross could find but little pleasure in such an indulgence.

A father is an ink renderer working for an inadequate

salary. If he could take a course in drafting, he would make more money. He saves from his lunch money. Just as he has acquired enough for the course, Muriel, age six, gets bad tonsils. The doctor says they must come out. Daddy remains an ink renderer for another three years.

Father needs a new tool. Mother needs a new coat. The children need new shoes. The children get the shoes. Father gets a headache. Mother gets the once-over at Sunday Mass.

I have made no reference here to families who have more than they need, or to those whose needs are always adequately cared for. Such families, to practise poverty, must go outside the family. In most cases justice, not charity, demands this. It isn't hard to find someone who needs what you have in abundance. You usually sit beside such a person at Sunday Mass.

We can presuppose that a Christian family grows normally in children planned *for* and not *against*. Few enterprises receive less encouragement. Not even the founding of a religious order goes so unapplauded or unaided by a secular world as does the maintenance of a large working-class family. Since this is the case, the poverty of such a family must be ingenious. In every way the parents must try to provide by their own labors the necessities they cannot afford at the stores. The things they must buy require a mastery of the art of bargain-hunting to pay as little as possible for the best quality.

A few yards of muslin and some boxes of dye provide cheerful draperies for the living-room windows. A bit of skill with tools and a trip to the distributors replaces a cracked hinge on the refrigerator at a small fraction of the cost of having it serviced. A set of second-hand clippers prevents a clipping at the hands of the local barber every time the kids become shaggy. A few extra dollars spent at the right time for vegetables in quantity, to store or can, means a saving over a period of months. A cobbler's last comes in handy. A woman needs a good sewing machine. Practical nursing and an eye for symptoms keeps the doctor away except in serious cases.

What, you may ask, has all this got to do with poverty? Tools and skills are, in fact, riches, perhaps the only kind of material riches. Then why call it poverty? The poverty lies in the denial of luxuries, pleasures, rest, and comfort that must be made in order to purchase the tools and use them. You can't sit down and listen to "Inner Sanctum Mysteries" while there are two chairs to be mended. It is something to forego the ingratiating courtesies of the "Nice Store" clerks in order to crawl with the rest of the proletariat through mounds of goods on the bargain counter. You continue to wear the same shabby suit so that you can afford some plumbing tools. You work at the sewing machine until well after midnight when there are no tiny hands to get at the thread. For her birthday Mother gets a new pump for the antiquated washer. For his birthday Daddy gets a brace and bit so that he can re-assemble the kitchen furniture. The price of *Theology and Sanity* is expended on yardgoods for Junior's coat. The cost of a night-out is represented in the new paint-job on the old crib for the new baby. This is ingenious poverty.

This point requires much more consideration than I can give it here. We have been acting on the fallacy that families exist in a vacuum. We have forgotten that a family must be part of a community of families. Being poor as a church mouse is tough on church mice because mice do not practise mutual charity. In the usual run of things deprivation and prosperity alternate in our lives. In a community it is seldom likely that everyone will be impoverished or, at least, be without the same things at the same time. This fluctuation in affluence is the natural occasion for neighborliness. "What have I got that you need, what have you got that I need?"

We must rebuild communities within and without the cities by reviving the economic system of mutual charity. This is already being done in many places. The breakdown of our present economy (an economy that cannot provide homes or decent food *is* broken down) is having the providential effect of throwing people together in mutual co-operation. Since every family, especially the father, should be engaged in restoring the community, holy poverty in our times must be communal.

All those who are convinced of the need for inter-family co-operation will, as soon as they act upon it, discover that they must deny themselves certain pleasures, wealth, and comforts so that they can work with others to build homes, organize co-operatives, sponsor parochial units, found maternity guilds, operate family services, attend retreats and study meetings, aid the stricken, shoulder the burdens of the fallen . . . and so on, endlessly, practising denial *as a family* so that the instrument of the family will be preserved.

It would seem that the very wolves that snap at the flanks of the family are those extremely useful crosses that must go with family life. The constant demands for food, clothing, and shelter, the bearing with sickness, weakness, and death, are the scourging disciplines that make the parent lean and trim to run so as to win. The firm demands of circumstance serve the same purpose in the married state as the rigorous rule provides for the monastic.

Though the poverty (as I have defined it) must be measured and planned, there is no way of avoiding the unforeseen crosses to which the family in particular is prey. It stands to reason, then, that all voluntary deprivations serve their best purpose, not in merely clearing the decks for action, but in disciplining the will to do the Will of God. If we deny ourselves the things we could have (the night-out for the new crib), then it will be easier for us to accept graciously the trials we cannot avoid. Voluntary poverty must be patient or else it will be no more than stoicism or human competence. The plan will become everything. We will become poverty snobs. In the name of thrift we will become misers. We will be as proud of what we *do* as the bourgeois are about what they *have*.

Austerity is not virtue. It is merely the soil in which virtue will grow if grace plants the seed, and Christ brings it to fruit.

Date Due

Ar4'59			
C. P. M.			
Mr 12			

Demco 293-5